CAR TROUBLE

CAR TROUBLE

A CHILDHOOD ON FOUR WHEELS

WENSLEY CLARKSON

MAINSTREAM
PUBLISHING

EDINBURGH AND LONDON

First published in Great Britain in 2010 by
MAINSTREAM PUBLISHING COMPANY
(EDINBURGH) LTD
7 Albany Street
Edinburgh EH1 3UG

ISBN 9781845966126

This book is a work of non-fiction based on the life, experiences
and recollections of the author. In some cases, names of people, places, dates,
sequences or the detail of events have been changed to protect
the privacy of others. The author has stated to the publishers that,
except in such respects not affecting the substantial accuracy of
the work, the contents of this book are true

Illustrations © Michael Osborne

Grateful acknowledgement is made for permission to reprint the following lyrics
in this volume: on p. 11 'My Mother the Car' by Paul Hampton (1965), © Paul
Hampton, reproduced by permission of Alfred Publishing Co., Inc.; on p. 26
'I Can't Stop Loving You' by Ray Charles (1962), © Don Gibson, reproduced
by permission of Sony/ATV Music Publishing (UK) Limited; on p. 63 'Waiting
for Your Taxi' by Ian Dury and The Blockheads (1979), © Ian Dury and Chas
Jankel, reproduced by permission of Helene Blue Musique Ltd

A catalogue record for this book is available from the British Library

Typeset in Sabon

Printed and bound in Great Britain by
CPI Mackays, Chatham, ME5 8TD

1 3 5 7 9 10 8 6 4 2

This book can only be dedicated to Pam and Tony Clarkson in the hope they are looking down from that drive-in pub in the sky.

'Loneliness adds beauty to life. It puts a special burn on sunsets and makes night air smell better.'

Henry Rollins

PSST . . .

AS A CHILD, I ALWAYS ENJOYED KEEPING SECRETS. THEY empowered me in a sense because they made me feel that I had some advantage over the people around me.

No one has ever talked about my biggest secret because I am the only one who knows the full story of it. That makes it a very emotional secret, like knowing something about your parents that they might wish you not to know or seeing something that you shouldn't see which then has to be kept a secret. We've all got loads of them.

While bouncing certain aspects of this book off my closest friends and colleagues, I've noticed that my particular secret relates closely to many other people's childhoods as well as mine.

So that's why I have decided to reveal it here in this book.

Obviously I wasn't born with it inside me, but it's certainly been with me since an early age. But I only realised the full significance of it all when I first began thinking about writing a book about my strange childhood.

According to the dictionary, an obsession is: '1. A compulsive preoccupation with a fixed idea or an unwanted feeling or emotion, often accompanied by symptoms of anxiety. 2. A compulsive, often unreasonable idea or emotion.'

CAR TROUBLE

That sums it all up perfectly because this secret obsession of mine has crossed many boundaries in my life and could frequently have ended in death and disaster.

No doubt you have noticed that I have not actually told you what that secret obsession is yet. I haven't even properly alluded to it, although the title of this book probably gives it away.

Anyway, here's my story and I'm sticking to it!

AUTHOR'S NOTE

I DON'T BELIEVE IN TALKING EVERYTHING THROUGH AND trying to blame the past for the present. I've always respected a person's right *not* to mention such things and how it is vital to get on with your life, without worrying about what happened years ago. So when you read this account of my childhood, remember this is not an excuse for who I am. It *is* who I am. I would not be here writing about my love affair with four wheels if it were not for my charming, reckless, affectionate and impulsive parents, who encouraged me to drive at such a ridiculously young age.

Oh, and before I forget, here's an important note to younger readers: please do not try this at home. The rules and regulations about driving have tightened up considerably since I was a kid and you'd *never* get away with it these days.

Wensley Clarkson, 2010

Believe it or not my mother dear decided she'd come back.
As a car.
She's my very own guiding star.
That's my mother dear.

'My Mother the Car'
Paul Hampton

DECEMBER 1996

'NURSE. NURSE. THIS IS MY SON. HE MAKES HIS LIVING FROM murders.'

It was a strange thing for a mother to say about her son, especially when she was lying on her deathbed in a musty-smelling hospice at the time. But the nurse was so busy she didn't take a blind bit of notice of the old lady with the sinister gap between her front teeth, lying flat on her back, sweating profusely on a bed with a 'Nil By Mouth' clipboard hanging on it.

My mother undoubtedly enjoyed making me sound more like a criminal than someone who writes books about them, but then she was a 77-year-old woman whose favourite song was 'Golden Brown' by The Stranglers. I managed to smile down at her that morning. In her mind, she was on the verge of completing her last ever journey.

'Come here,' she whispered hoarsely, in her uniquely masculine smoker's drawl.

As I leaned down and kissed her reluctantly on the forehead, she pushed a wet flannel into my hand and forced me to mop her brow. She was burning hot and shaking like a leaf. As I began wiping the sweat away, my movements gradually seemed to find a rhythm and she started visibly relaxing. Then she looked up at me. The yellowing whites of her eyes contrasted starkly with the bluey-grey pupils that were now locked on the neon strip lights in the ceiling. That old sparkle had long gone.

At first I'd felt awkward, standing there in the ward pressing the flannel up against her forehead, but the longer I did it, the easier it became. I tried to keep smiling while I looked down at her, but it was hard to put any real warmth into it. I'd always felt such a wide range of emotions when it came to my mother.

Suddenly, her clammy hand clamped itself around my wrist to stop me wiping away her sweat. 'I want you to have the Mercedes. You've always liked driving it.'

Hmmmm. My mother's Mercedes 450SL drove a bit like a lumbersome speedboat. The air conditioning sounded like Bernard Manning crouched behind the dashboard playing blow football, but it was one hell of a car.

For a few seconds, I made no attempt to pull my hand away or react to what she'd just said. Her comment had come completely out of left field. I just let her hang on to me. Then I looked down at her and she seemed to be staring into me with an almost childlike, appealing expression.

'It's time,' she whispered. 'Time to go now. I'm ready.'

I had to stop and think what she meant by that.

Her hand was still clamped around my wrist. She made a weak attempt to squeeze it tighter.

'Come on,' she urged. 'Just push the flannel hard over my face. It won't take long.'

I knew then exactly what she wanted me to do.

Nothing much had changed. My mother needed me to come to her rescue, knowing full well that she was about to drive off without me yet again.

THIS IS THE FIRST PART!

My driving debut.

RUST-BUCKET WITH CHARM

I AM SITTING ON THE EDGE OF A LITTLE ROWING BOAT, LEANING precariously into the oily water, trying to grab at a turquoise-coloured, rusting Riley 1.5 Matchbox toy car that is floating on a tiny piece of wood on the surface. My father is also trying to reach it, but that is making the boat topple even further into the water and I am scared. Scared that we will fall into the smelly, greasy Thames, but even more scared that my little car – my favourite toy – is about to sink beneath the surface. My father has had a couple of gins and at least half a bottle of wine, so I am also scared that he'll fall in and drown.

I am close to tears. I look up at his bloodshot eyes and try to force a smile. He looks down at me and then tries one last time to stretch out of the boat and across the water to rescue my car.

Maybe I was three, possibly even younger. It was 1959, and toy cars were my obsession and would remain that way until they were replaced by the real thing. Castro had taken over Cuba that year. Cecil B. de Mille died, but most important of all one of my favourite TV series, *Bonanza*, had just begun its fifteen-year run. Obviously I didn't know all this stuff when I was three, but looking back on it I was lucky to be born into a reasonably well-off family, even though they spent more time partying than parenting.

CAR TROUBLE

As I sat back on the edge of that boat and tried not to look at my beloved Riley floating amongst the sewage in the polluted River Thames, I felt the boat rock alarmingly. Then my father, sitting behind me, pulled his soaking arm out of the river and I felt the water dripping on my neck. I turned back, expecting to see my little car sinking into the river, but it had already disappeared beneath the surface. I was crestfallen. I sat back on the side of the boat without even looking up at my father as the tears began streaming down my face.

Just then he pushed a clenched fist gently up against my tummy. Was he angry over something? Why was he doing that? He pressed his fist tighter into my stomach. Then I looked up and saw him smiling as his hand began to open. That tiny toy car was in his palm. 'There you go. I told you to trust me and I'd get it out for you.'

Funny how the turquoise paint job on that little toy Riley has stuck in my mind while the faces of the important adults in my life have become hazy, their features blurring into one another, always smiling as long as they had a drink in their hands. I suppose that was my earliest childhood memory, lodging in my mind for two important reasons – because it was one of the few occasions where trust in an adult turned out not to be misplaced, and because it marked the beginning of an obsession with cars that would last throughout my childhood . . .

THE STARTING GRID

EVERYONE IN THE STREET WHERE WE LIVED IN UPMARKET Kensington, West London, seemed to be either a lawyer or a doctor, except my father, who was a Fleet Street tabloid journalist. And although we lived in the biggest house in our road, we were definitely the poorest residents.

That's because my mother had bought the house on the cheap as it was filled to the brim with sitting tenants. My tiny bedroom on the top floor was jammed between an 80-year-old ex-brothel madam, an elderly maths teacher and a French lady who was always bringing strange men back to her room. We all shared the same bathroom. In the basement were two more bedsits, with more sitting tenants. We were literally sandwiched between all these strangers.

Elsewhere in the street, the neighbourhood wives got on with their domestic chores while their rich and successful husbands went off and earned big salaries. The housewives all nodded to each other in the street and held sherry parties just before Christmas every year. But my mother never made it onto their invitation lists, although that's not surprising since – like most French people – she didn't do small talk. She wasn't too keen on cooking, either, which wasn't so typically French. When my father got home at about eight most nights, it was my job from a young age to pour them both a Gordon's gin and water, no ice, no slice of lemon. I sneaked a taste one time and it put me off gin for life.

The house we lived in was vast, dusty and very draughty. But outside there were lots of trees in the street, which showered blossom in spring, although my mother didn't notice it much because she often stayed in bed all day. It was like that for many years before and after I was born. My mother just didn't like opening the curtains some mornings, even after I took her up a nice hot cup of Nescafé instant coffee. It was only later that I realised those strange-looking blue-and-red tablets on her bedside table were Tuinal tranquillisers, given to her by her doctor to dull some private pain and heartache that I was never allowed to see.

My parents were probably the most unpopular people in our stuffy street because our stucco-fronted house was unpainted, the fencing was falling apart and the hedge was lucky to get a trim once a year. Next door on one side were five new houses all built after Hitler's bombs flattened the previous homes. Most weekday mornings the husbands appeared in their pinstripe suits and bowler hats and marched off to their important jobs. The houses on the opposite side of the road were much older Victorian properties, mainly split up into flats. My bedroom looked straight out onto them and I'd spend hours watching all their inhabitants' movements and working out what cars they drove. Goodness knows what the rest of the street thought of us and our hatful of sitting tenants, who'd come and go at all times of the day and night.

The rear garden of the house backed onto the main refuse depot of the Royal Borough of Kensington and Chelsea, which was the other reason why my parents were able to afford this four-storey mansion in the first place. It was hardly what estate agents would call a 'desirable location', with the smell of rotting rubbish drifting through the air and Bedford seven-ton refuse lorries grinding their gears and letting out their air-brakes, which hissed loudly like giant vipers.

Up in my tiny bedroom at the top of the house, loads of raggedy, fat, noisy pigeons regularly perched on my window ledge when I left out breadcrumbs for them. I liked the pigeons because they kept me company when I was on my own, which was a lot of the time.

It was the late 1950s and the air was still thick with smog, even though everyone was supposed to be burning only smokeless coal in their fireplaces. My mother used the outside cold as an excuse to stay in bed all day, and she liked to remind me how her childhood in the 1920s and 1930s was spent in the south of France, where there was *no* smog and a lot of sunshine. My mother also mentioned how she had had servants when she was my age. Maybe that's why she liked me to wait on her hand and foot? But I didn't mind because I liked being needed around the house and having a sense of purpose.

During winter my mother would venture out of bed to the kitchen to make herself a drink, push a ten-bob note into my hand and ask me to pop round to the corner shop to pick her up a couple of packs of Benson & Hedges. Sometimes I got lucky and she'd be tipsy enough by the time I got back to have forgotten how much she had given me in the first place. I don't think she cared whether I nicked the odd bob or two. And even if she ever mentioned her suspicions to my father, he wouldn't have punished me because he was as soft as butter. All I wanted was enough money to buy my favourite model cars from the toyshop at the end of the road.

In the summer, my mother would often appear in our back garden overlooked by the council refuse dump, strip down to a sparkling gold bikini and start sunbathing as if her life depended on it. She'd lie on a red plastic sunlounger slap bang in the middle of the garden, chain-smoking and smothering herself in coconut oil, which would sizzle after about five minutes. She even had one of those silver-foil reflector things round her neck so she could also get a tan under her chin. It all put me off sunbathing for life.

There are these really cheesy photos of me taken in the garden at that time with my mother tanning away in the background while I charge wildly around in a scaled-down version of an Austin A40 just big enough for me to squeeze into. It was made out of tin and had pedals. On the very first afternoon I got it, I almost knocked down a granny while frantically steering it up and down the pavement outside our house.

My mother loved pulling those photos out of a drawer in the kitchen and showing them to friends and relatives because I actually looked happy in them. But that was only because it was the first time I'd ever got behind the wheel of a car. I've never forgotten the excited knot in my tummy as I pumped away furiously on the pedals to bring the car up to its top speed of 2 or 3 mph. The floor of my powder-blue A40 eventually rotted right through, leaving my sandals scraping the tarmac, a bit like Fred in *The Flintstones*. But at least it never ran out of petrol.

Every night I placed my three favourite toy cars on the bed, next to my pillow, along with my pale-blue Austin on the floor alongside me. That old rusting turquoise Matchbox Riley my father rescued from the river took pride of place, even though the other three cars were much more expensive Corgis.

I often had a dream in which my mother and father were stranded on a busy roundabout at the start of the A3 dual carriageway, near Richmond Park. I'd drive my little tin Austin up onto that roundabout, slam on the brakes and they'd jump in the back like a couple of naughty children. Then a white police Ford Zephyr, just like the ones they drove in *Z-Cars*, spotted us as I skidded off the grass verge and landed back on the road with a bump. A dramatic chase followed, but I always managed to get my parents home safely. My father would then proudly reward me with enough money to buy the latest Corgi car from the toyshop at the end of the road. Then I'd arrive at the toyshop only to find it had completely disappeared, and that's when I always woke up, relieved to find all four of my toy cars, including the Austin, still there in the morning where I had left them when I fell asleep.

From an early age I was more used to the company of grown-ups than children. I went with the flow and never really felt the need to ask many questions. But a lot of my time was spent up in my little bedroom avoiding my parents' strange world, unless, of course, there was a car involved.

In the middle of all this, my dear old dad remained a happy-go-lucky soul despite having an eccentric, reclusive drink- and prescription-drug-addicted wife and a car-obsessed little boy with a bad pudding-bowl haircut. My father didn't even seem to mind our house being full of sitting tenants. On the other hand, my mother always avoided the subject if any visitors asked whom these strange people were wandering through the house. Sometimes my dad made fun of her by saying my mother liked having company in the day, when he was away working long hours. My mother would then glare across at him and the subject was quickly dropped. My parents had this 'shorthand' between themselves, which seemed to involve ignoring each other completely when there was a problem or giving out a look of unreserved contempt.

RAY CHARLES & THE ZODIAC

MY FATHER HAD BEEN A COMMUNIST BEFORE THE WAR, LIKE many other journalists on the *Daily Mirror*. But he never once tried to thrust his beliefs down anyone's throat and got fed up of it in the end. He also wasn't too keen on knocking on doors as a reporter so he used his undoubted tact and ambition to rapidly climb the ladder into management. My father was a master at not confronting trouble, especially when it came to my mother.

He also had a certain style to him; his shirts were nearly always white and crisp and his suits double-breasted and baggy. He was a ruggedly good-looking fellow with swept-back black hair and a long, straight nose. One of his oldest friends later described him as looking a bit like a Mafia don, except that he came from New Zealand not Sicily. He had that classic look of men in the 1950s and early 1960s, a cross between famous London gangster boss Jack Spot and Prime Minister Harold Macmillan.

But my father's long work hours certainly didn't help improve my mother's state of mind. One morning when he went off for yet another eighteen-hour stint at the newspaper office, she shut herself away in the bedroom and started playing Ray Charles' classic 'I Can't Stop Loving You' over and over and over again on her gramophone player. Up in my tiny bedroom, I soon learned the words off by heart:

CAR TROUBLE

I can't stop loving you
I've made up my mind
To live in memory of the lonesome times
I can't stop wanting you
It's useless to say
So I'll just live my life in dreams of yesterday

I stayed in my bedroom all that day – hemmed in, as usual, by sitting tenants – because I didn't want to invade my mother's space. I knew she was on the verge of doing something really mad. In any case, I'd just invented my own game, noting down in my exercise book the makes of different cars whizzing past our house. It proved the perfect diversion that day. Later that evening I heard my father struggling up the stairs. No doubt he'd had a boozy lunch plus a couple of 'liveners' before leaving the office. That Ray Charles track was still playing over and over.

My father wasn't a violent drunk. Actually, he seemed even happier when he was under the influence. But moments after he arrived home that night, there was a lot of shouting and swearing. I crept down to the half floor – where the bathroom I shared with the tenants was located – and crouched down to look between the banisters. One of the tenants, the elderly spinster called Miss Hogg, came out of her door and glanced down at me before going back into her room. I think she'd heard it all before.

Meanwhile, Ray Charles was still belting out his song for at least the 50th time that day:

Those happy hours that we once knew
Tho' long ago, they still make me blue
They say that time heals a broken heart
But time has stood still since we've been apart

Suddenly Ray Charles' voice was sliced in half by the sound of the needle scratching right through the middle of the track. It gave me the fright of my life. An eerie few beats of silence followed. Then I heard the window being ripped open. A split second more of silence, then a huge crash as something hit the pavement in front of the house. I darted back up the stairway to my bedroom and rushed straight to the window to see the remnants of my mother's shattered record player lying in pieces on the pathway right in front of our gleaming two-tone, sky-blue-and-grey Ford Zodiac Mark II. Thank God it wasn't damaged. I washed that car every Sunday like clockwork. It was *my* pride and joy.

Seconds later I heard the front door slam and watched from the window as my father stomped up the street, still dressed in his suit and mac. I pressed my face hard against the glass, worried that if I took my eyes off him, he might disappear. I hoped he'd turn round and come back. But he didn't.

I sat there still looking through the window for at least five minutes after my father disappeared that evening. Then a beautiful metallic-blue Bristol 405 came gliding gracefully down our street. I grabbed my exercise book and scribbled down its details. It was such a relief to think about cars again. They seemed much nicer than people.

My mother didn't emerge from the bedroom so that evening I cooked myself a couple of bangers under the grill. Later, back once again in my tiny bedroom, I started flicking aimlessly through my favourite book at the time, *The Ladybird Book of Motor Cars*. It was full of huge, ugly lumps of metal like the Austin Cambridge estate and the Morris Minor, and then I got to page 32 and the Mercedes 280SE 3.5. For me as a little kid, this motor car with its distinctive-looking stacked headlights was kind of like having *Bonanza* and *Thunderbirds* all rolled up together into one TV programme. With a Vulcan jet bomber swooping over the Ponderosa as the aquatic *Thunderbird 4* emerged majestically from the surface of a nearby lake. Oh. And lots of chocolate flakes sticking out of a mound of Wall's bright-yellow vanilla ice cream.

THE LOGBOOK

IF THERE WERE A BUDGET OR AN ELECTION OR A BANK holiday, then my parents would host a party to celebrate it. They surrounded themselves with other people to help paper over the cracks in their own relationship. I'd watch their guests arrive from my bedroom window as they parked up in their big saloon cars and note down all the models and registration numbers in a special logbook. Then I'd slip quietly down to the top of the first flight of stairs, where I'd crouch by the banisters in my pyjamas, which were usually pale blue and always covered in a toy-car pattern. I'd strain to listen to all their laughing and joking, while not really understanding much of what they were saying.

From the age of five I was allowed to make an early evening appearance at these parties, where many of my parents' friends would push a shilling or a sixpence in my hand, as I was the only child present. I became highly skilled at charming the adults to get enough money to run up the road to that toyshop on the corner and buy yet another Dinky or Corgi car. I'd stopped collecting the cheaper, smaller Matchbox models on my fifth birthday. Then I'd retreat back into my strange little world at the top of the house. I remember all the toy cars I bought at that time far more clearly than the names and faces of the guests at my parents' parties.

CAR TROUBLE

They were a mixture of journalists, actors, businessmen and writers. One of my father's best friends, a well-known author, locked himself in the loo one night and refused to come out for a day and a half because he was working out a new plot for a novel. I can't remember much else about him, except that he didn't drive.

My father always enjoyed having these parties, while my mother veered from getting on far too well with some guests to retiring early to her bed with a bored expression on her face. She liked to be the centre of attention and, although over 40 years of age, always dressed in glamorous, quite tight-fitting clothes. Most of the time her head was completely in the clouds and she'd look straight through people if she couldn't be bothered to hear or speak to them. Then she'd go all glassy-eyed and assume a false smile that was quite startling due to the large gap between her two front teeth. Her hair was classic south-of-France peroxide blonde, and she always had jangling gold bracelets on both wrists, which complemented the look of a tall, willowy fading film star rather like the mysterious and sad Norma Desmond from *Sunset Boulevard*.

During one party I walked into the kitchen and found her kissing another woman full on the lips. She didn't even bother to stop when I appeared at the door. She knew I'd turn round and leave, rather like a father who's walked in on his daughter's first snog. And that's exactly what I did. The only thing I remember about that other woman was that her husband drove an impressive-looking Wolseley 6/110, the same model that New Scotland Yard used to chase bank robbers.

I was already becoming the parent to my own parents. But then it wasn't difficult to be the sensible one, compared to my mother and father.

MAGICAL DRIVE TO WATERLOO BRIDGE

IT WAS A RAINY, EARLY MORNING SOME TIME DURING THE autumn of 1962 and the Cuban Missile Crisis that October threatened the future of the world. But I was more concerned by my new prep school, which was run by an evil headmaster who caned me on the hand most weeks for insubordination. I was trying not to breathe heavily, but I could hear myself so clearly it was making me feel really nervous. Suddenly, I recognised my father's favourite dark-brown suede shoes walking down the front steps of our house. He was perilously close to where I was hiding – on the floor of the back-seat area of our two-tone Ford Zodiac parked in front of the house.

'Where the hell is he?' asked my father as he turned to my mother, who was standing at the front door in a faded pink dressing gown. My mother didn't reply, but then she rarely responded to direct questions from my father.

'He'll turn up soon, I suppose. Just make sure he gets to school, okay?'

Again, no reaction from my mother. The front door slammed shut. I felt a pang of guilt, as I'd always liked walking to school with my father, especially when we played this game called 'Capital Cities' in which we went through every one in the world.

I hated my new school so much I'd been up half the night thinking of a way to avoid going. Then just before daylight, I'd slid into the car while my mother and father were still asleep. I knew that once he'd gone to work I'd be in the clear.

So, after hearing the front door slam, I waited a few moments in case he'd forgotten something and then emerged from my little hiding place in the Zodiac and quietly shut the car's back door. My mother was in the kitchen as I crept in, but all she did was calmly look up at me, nod and then smile. It was oddly reassuring, even though I knew from the vacant expression on her face she was in another world, fuelled by tranquillisers. I took the *Daily Mirror* from the hall table and headed up to my bedroom. I learned more from reading that newspaper, watching the TV news and playing Capital Cities with my dad than just about anything at school.

My mother didn't want to be alone all day so in a sense she was rewarding me with this freedom. She *never* pried into my business, just as I hadn't asked her what she was up to when she was kissing that woman.

I never found out until many years later what had turned her into this strange, distant creature. She'd had another child three years before I was born. But one morning she went into the nursery to get her eighteen-month-old baby son Nicholas up and found him dead, his head twisted between the bars of his cot. He'd died trying to get his head back out from between those bars. My mother never fully recovered and remained haunted by what had happened to her baby for the rest of her life.

She drank and smoked very heavily while expecting me, but I survived so she can't have been that bad a mother. I don't even know what time I was born or how much I weighed, but one of my relatives let slip years later that my mother handed me over to the nurse within seconds of my birth because she couldn't handle the fear that she might drop me.

It wasn't until I turned five years of age that my mother began properly venturing out into the world again, leaving me spending even more time alone in our house with only the sitting tenants for company. While she was out, I'd busy myself up in my bedroom for hours on end, scribbling down the names of the cars and lorries driving by on the street below as I waited for her to return home.

I learned about virtually every make and model of vehicle on the road. I became obsessed with noting down even the smallest changes between models. Did you know the only difference between a Triumph 2000 and a Triumph 2.5PI was a narrow matt strip on the rear of the 2.5PI? I even gave certain cars their own nicknames after their grilles because so many of them were like faces staring straight at you.

I later added up a total of thirty thousand vehicles, which had passed our house between the ages of six and eleven. At the end of each day I examined the notes in my red exercise book to calculate which make of car had passed the house the most times and then I'd award it a gold star. At the end of every month I gave out an award to the car that had won the most gold stars.

Throwing myself into my hobby helped me stop worrying so much about where my mother was. While she was out, I'd let out a disappointed sigh whenever a car drove around the bend in our street and turned out not to be her. I even developed a habit of gnawing on the skin around my thumbs while I sat waiting and waiting. Eventually, her Zodiac with the ferocious chrome front grille careered around the corner, mounted the pavement and narrowly missed a pedestrian or two before it slammed to a halt in the compact carport in the front garden of our house. My mother then emerged, crashing the driver's door shut behind her at least twice to make sure it was properly closed but never remembering to lock it. I'd rush down the stairs to greet her as she stumbled up the steps into the house. She'd usually flop straight into bed. I'd always make sure she was covered with a blanket to keep her warm.

Then I'd slip quietly out of the front door and slide ever so casually into the Zodiac and pretend to drive it. Pedestrians would stroll by, trying hard to ignore the silly little boy furiously threading the steering wheel from right to left and back again, while making ludicrous *broooom broooom* car-engine noises.

CAR TROUBLE

Then my father would arrive home. He'd usually be in a good mood after a few drinks at work and not even particularly surprised to see his son jumping around in his company car like a demented Stirling Moss. Maybe he thought I was better off in the driving seat of the Zodiac than inside that strange house?

One time, my father was in such a jolly mood that he got in the front of the car with me and I pretended to drive him to his office in Stamford Street, near Waterloo Bridge. He gave me precise directions as I 'chauffeured' him. Then, before leaving his imaginary office to come home, I tried to make him take the wheel and he admitted for the first time that he hadn't driven since the Second World War, when his amphibious vehicle (they were known as 'Army Ducks') came under fire during the troop landings in Normandy in 1944. I even offered to teach him how to drive, but he didn't want to be reminded of his war experiences and turned down my kind offer. No wonder he left the real driving to my mother.

She drove without any fear whatsoever. She was brilliant at judging spaces and overtaking at just the right moment, even on narrow roads. She rarely used the car's indicators and ignored most red lights, but, typically, she always seemed to get away with breaking all the rules.

EL MINX!

MY MOTHER'S MAIDEN NAME WAS 'MINCK' SO SHE COULDN'T resist borrowing her best friend's Hillman Super 'Minx' Convertible sometimes. With canary-yellow bodywork and an immaculate leatherette white hood, I tried to imagine it was a Cadillac convertible, but there was one big difference: 0–60 in ten minutes. Although it did only cost eight hundred quid brand new.

One time, when I was about five years old, my mother borrowed the Minx convertible and announced we were off on a family holiday to Spain in it. She thought being in a soft top in the sweltering heat would be more fun, I guess. For some eccentric reason that I never fully worked out, we took the Minx on a train from Calais to southern France and then drove into Spain from there.

I don't remember much about the train journey, but that's no big surprise because it's the driving part of my childhood that's usually etched the most on my mind. The first memory of that holiday was of my mother unpeeling her brown-suede-and-beige-crocheted driving gloves in the searing heat to give some sweaty-looking Spanish Guardia Civil officer our passports at the border crossing with France. They had those funny black-patent hats, which looked like something one of my wooden toy soldiers might wear. But the Guardia Civil cop looked much meaner and nastier than any toy I owned. He snatched the passports and spent ages inspecting them while walking around the Minx. He seemed very irritated by a woman at the wheel and was also looking accusingly at my father for being such wimp because he was not the driver. My father looked very nervous of the paramilitaries because this was the first time he'd been back in Spain since the Civil War and these Guardia Civil were Franco's own personal police force. In other words, they had been his enemy just over 20 years earlier.

But it was the Minx that attracted the most attention. It was such a quintessentially English saloon car with its narrow tyres, straight lines and narrow, flat-faced chrome grille, yet it was also a convertible.

In the end, my dad the seasoned traveller managed to avoid trouble the only way he knew how: by bunging the cop a 100-peseta note. The Guardia Civil officers were obsessed with where we were travelling, and my dad gave them the name of a hotel near where we were going, even though we were actually staying with one of his best friends from the Civil War, a writer called Steve Francis, who had fought alongside my father against the very people who were now inspecting the Minx. Francis lived in the coastal town of Rosas, just north of Barcelona, and after staying with him we'd be heading further down the east coast to visit some other old pals of my father's from the Civil War's International Brigade. Many of them had stayed on after losing the war and married beautiful Spanish women half their age. I sometimes wondered if my dad regretted missing out on a life in the Spanish sunshine that he so adored.

I was fascinated by driving abroad, which was potentially bloody dangerous with my mother on the 'wrong' side of the road, although I don't recall any near misses during that trip. The visit also fuelled my lifelong interest in Spain.

HORSE AND PARENT TRAP

BUT NOT ALL MY MEMORIES OF THAT TRIP TO SPAIN REVOLVE around my mother's driving skills. A few days after visiting my father's friend Steve Francis in Rosas, I came to find myself all alone, walking through the blisteringly dry Mediterranean heat, surrounded by hundreds upon hundreds of olive trees. Shaking with fear, I was completely lost and utterly convinced I would never see my mother and father again.

My parents had earlier been having one of their typically intense, booze-fuelled conversations while we were being driven in a tourist horse and carriage with jingling bells, around the edge of Valencia. I loathed that old-fashioned contraption. I'd much rather have gone out in one of those sleek-looking black-and-yellow SEAT taxicabs with the straight lines and triangular rear tail fins. Instead, I was sitting in that decrepit horse and carriage in a right strop. Thanks in part to their liberal intake of booze, my parents had always been surprisingly good at ignoring my ridiculous temper tantrums. They didn't get tense like normal parents, and most of the time they just laughed at my ludicrous foot-stamping behaviour.

But I was so infuriated that day that when the horse and carriage stopped to allow a tractor to drive across the road, I jumped off without saying a word. They just carried on and I wasn't even sure if they'd noticed I had gone. I only began to worry when the horse and carriage disappeared around the bend. For ages, I just stood there waiting for them to come back.

For the next two hours I found myself wandering aimlessly around in blistering temperatures in what seemed like a maze of olive trees. The mid-afternoon sun was beating down on my head and I felt dizzy and dehydrated. I'd started sobbing an hour earlier when it dawned on me that maybe they weren't going to come back at all. I had no water and no idea where I was, and I started to wonder if my life was about to end.

Then I spotted something in the distance. The heat haze meant it was impossible to make out *who* it was, but a black figure was definitely coming towards me. I squinted and tried to concentrate, but for the moment it wasn't any clearer so I just kept walking.

It gradually turned out to be an old man in a black beret. I was painfully shy but decided to summon up the courage to stop him and ask for help. As he got closer, sweat poured down my face. It wasn't just the heat, either, but the sheer panic of having to talk to a complete stranger. I was still looking down onto the dusty road at this stage, afraid of looking up and shouting at the old man in case he turned around and disappeared. I could hear his boots scuffing the dusty track, getting closer and closer.

Then I glanced up hesitantly, hoping to catch his eye. But he was looking away in the direction of the olive groves and didn't even acknowledge my presence. I took a deep breath and tried to say something, but my throat was bone dry and felt like sticky sandpaper. Then everything went quiet.

By the time I dared look up again, he'd completely disappeared down a side track. I'd missed my chance. Close to collapse, I stopped by the side of the road and sat down in a dry, dusty ditch under the shadow of an overhanging olive tree. I could not go any further. My legs ached and my hands were shaking.

I must have nodded off then because my next memory is of being suddenly awoken by the noise of a squeaky car suspension as it bounced along the dusty track somewhere nearby. For a split second I didn't know where I was. I still hadn't dared open my eyes. Finally,

I blinked into the searing sunlight and saw a black-and-yellow SEAT taxi charging straight towards me. Terrified, I stood up and jumped over a wall behind me in case it hit me. The taxi screeched to a halt just a couple of feet from me, throwing up huge clouds of dust as the back door flew open. Inside were my parents, looking at me with broad smiles across both their drunken faces.

'Well, well, well. Look who we've found,' said my mother, slightly slurring her words. 'Shall we give him a ride or let him make his own way back?'

I glanced nervously across at my father, who looked as if he felt sorry for me, but then he smiled at my mother so she wouldn't realise what he was thinking. At that moment I knew it was always going to be them against me. I couldn't really trust them. Everyone always lets you down in the end.

But at least I wouldn't have to sit in that bloody embarrassing horse and carriage ever again. On the way back to the hotel, my mother told me how they'd seriously thought about leaving me out there for at least another couple of hours to teach me a lesson for running away. But I didn't really care what she was saying by this stage; I was more interested in watching the greasy-haired taxi driver with a droopy moustache swerving around corners with a cigarette hanging out of his mouth as he gesticulated wildly to my irritated father about the talents of General Franco. Then I switched my attention to the column gear change on the SEAT. It reminded me of my mother's two-tone Ford Zodiac, back in London, as well as my beloved toy steering wheel, which I'd also left behind in London, much to my annoyance.

WHEEL-SPINNING IN THE DUST

A COUPLE OF DAYS AFTER QUITE HAPPILY LOSING ME IN THAT vast olive grove, my mother and father set off from Valencia to visit another of his old friends from the Spanish Civil War, who lived further south, near Alicante. My mum was still piloting that custard-yellow Hillman Minx convertible, and she'd promised I might get to steer the car on her lap if she found some wasteland out in the Spanish *campo*.

I'd been nagging her rather a lot to drive because I'd left that plastic stick-on steering wheel back in London and had already wasted half a day touring the toyshops of Barcelona trying to find an identical one, without success.

Just before we reached the outskirts of Alicante, my mother and father had a furious argument, which started when he switched the radio off because he was bored of the crap Spanish pop music that my mother seemed obsessed with listening to in order to avoid all issues, as usual. It was always the small things that kicked things off with them. I sat in the back curled up in a corner with my hands over my ears, humming to myself in the hope that by the time we arrived at my father's friend's house they would have stopped rowing. But having your hands over your ears doesn't really block much out, as any child will tell you. It just deepened the sounds of them arguing and in some ways made it all seem even more dramatic than it was. Every time I unclamped my hands from my ears their voices would cut right through me, and then I'd push the palms of my hands back over my ears and go back to the muffled version.

The next thing I knew, the Minx suddenly screeched to a halt and my father got out of the car and slammed the door behind him. I was quite relieved because it meant I was able to hear things normally again. I didn't even consider asking my mother what was happening. That remained one of our many unwritten rules.

The Minx sat there on the side of the dusty road for a few moments as my father stomped towards a small hotel that seemed to have a bar at the front of it, because a couple of locals with black berets were supping small glasses of beer in the blistering sunshine.

My mother just waited at the steering wheel. I could tell from the direction her head was pointing that she was watching him until he walked inside the hotel bar. Then she crunched the Minx into gear and we moved off. I was quite happy, in a twisted sort of way, because at least all the arguing had stopped.

Within seconds, I was thrown halfway across the back seat when she suddenly and quite angrily swept the car into the narrow entrance to an empty field right next to the same hotel where my father had just gone. I suppose you could call it a makeshift car park because there were a couple of scooters and a SEAT three-wheeler van parked up in one corner, next to a side entrance to the same hotel.

She slammed the brakes on in the middle of the field and churned up a cloud of thick dust. Then she yanked up the handbrake, before slowly unpeeling her brown-suede-and-beige-crocheted driving gloves, which she slapped down on the dashboard. Then she lit a cigarette. I presumed she'd turn off the engine and set off to the bar to see my dad. But instead she sat there, saying absolutely nothing, with the engine still running. I think she was expecting him to notice her and come running back, but my parents had a habit of challenging each other so this was going to be a long haul. My mother took a long, deep suck on her B&H and then got out of the Minx, with the engine still running, leaving me in the back seat.

She slammed the driver's door shut so hard that my father would have heard it from the hotel nearby. I noticed a couple of old women in black walking past, staring at us in the way they all did in Spain at the time. Mind you, my mother was dressed in a very bright orange dress, leaning against the front wing of the car, looking very agitated. Women dressed in anything other than black went against all the 'rules' of decency as far as the locals were concerned back then.

My mum turned, dropped her cigarette to the ground and stamped harshly on it with her heel. Then she leaned into the window on the driver's side. 'Come on then,' she said. I didn't know what she was on about at first.

But I noticed she kept glancing across at the hotel bar entrance. Obviously she was hoping my father was watching. I have no idea to this day if he was, but I do remember hearing a few kids shouting and the splash of water from a swimming pool in the grounds of the hotel, which distracted me a bit because I was still waiting for my mother to explain her earlier comment.

'Get in the front,' she said, never one for wasting words.

So I clambered into the front passenger seat of the Hillman Minx and waited for her to stop seething. I'm not sure exactly why, but I scanned around to make sure no one other than my mother was watching. The coast was clear, although she was still standing, with her arms crossed now, lighting up yet another cigarette. Oh, and I forgot to say earlier, she was wearing a floppy straw hat as well.

So here I was, too small to see properly through the windscreen, waiting for her to get in beside me for that driving lesson I'd been nagging her about since we left London. The Minx had a column gear change so just the idea of coordinating the clutch and accelerator was quite daunting, even though I'd avidly studied my mum and other drivers on the pedals since I was about three.

But she didn't get in beside me. Instead, she remained leaning against the car, arms crossed tensely and staring maniacally over towards the hotel bar.

I waited another minute, and then I thought that maybe she wanted me to try and drive the Minx on my own. I slid across the bench seat behind the cream-coloured steering wheel to see how she reacted. She was more interested in what was happening inside that bar.

CAR TROUBLE

The Minx engine was still running, but no one seemed in the slightest bit interested in either us or the car. My mum's B&H was sticking out of her mouth and no doubt her daily dose of Tuinal had kicked in hours earlier.

The moment I saw that glazed look in her eyes, I knew she was trying to put my dad through a form of torture because of the argument. But she was relying on the fact that he would be looking in our direction, and I was pretty sure he'd probably hidden himself in the far corner of that darkened bar.

I imagined putting the Minx into first gear so I pushed my foot down on the clutch and went into second, just the way I'd watched my mother and others do so many times in the past. But I couldn't quite summon up the courage to do it for real.

I loved being behind the wheel, but I needed a surge of confidence to run through my veins and it just wasn't there. Instead I was just very scared. Something was stopping me trying to drive the car for real. So I just sat there, mesmerised, with my foot stroking the accelerator, revving it up louder and louder but going nowhere fast.

I don't remember much of what happened after that, but my father later told me that I ended up going into the pool area behind the hotel for a swim because it was so hot. Apparently I jumped straight into the water, but then just sank like a stone to the bottom.

My next memory is of being dragged out of the water by a man who just happened to be there with his family. I didn't know where I was or what was going on.

He dragged me onto the side of the pool and pressed the palms of his hands very hard down on my stomach. I opened my eyes slowly and looked up to find my father peering anxiously down at me. He and my mother had been in the bar, knocking back endless drinks to 'celebrate' their reconciliation.

At that moment, my mother appeared, towering above me in her clickity-click heels. I could just make out her taking a huge drag of her cigarette before blowing smoke all over me, while uttering the immortal line: 'Thank God he knew how to swim.'

My father turned and looked at her as if she was completely stark staring mad. He wasn't such a bad judge of character after all.

That very first experience of being allowed to get properly behind the wheel of a car turned out to be my last for quite a while. That day my parents retreated back to the hotel bar, where they proceeded to drink the place dry and we were obliged to stay the night at the hotel so my mother could sleep it all off. That stupid argument they'd had earlier was soon forgotten in a haze of booze and cigarette smoke and tapas.

Looking back on it, I suppose I should be grateful that they weren't stressed by the fact I'd almost drowned. But then, on the other hand, maybe if they had been upset, it would have shown that they cared about the fact I nearly died partly because my mother was so off her head on tranquillisers that in order to punish her annoying husband, she'd almost let her five-year-old son drive her best friend's car.

DRINK-DRIVING ON COUNTRY LANES

A FEW MONTHS LATER, I WAS OUT 'DRIVING' WITH MY MOTHER IN the Surrey countryside. I say 'driving' because I'd stuck my special blue-and-white suction plastic toy steering wheel complete with column gear-change lever and a red hooter button onto the back of the Zodiac's grey-leather front-bench seat. And I was studiously aping every move my mother made for real up front.

Our Zodiac Mark II had a two-tone ice-cream paint job, white-wall tyres, spotlights and sharpened tail fins that narrowly avoided stabbing pedestrians whenever my mother reversed into them. It had a 2.5 straight-6 engine and its turning circle was virtually the same as the *Queen Mary* cruise liner.

Eventually that day we stopped at a pub, where my mother went in to meet a friend before bringing me out a bottle of pop and a packet of Smith's crisps, with the salt in a separate blue baggie. I must have sat there for at least two hours nursing that drink, watching all the other families out in the pub garden having a jolly time. But I wasn't jealous because I had the Zodiac all to myself and was sitting there behind the real steering wheel, driving it in my head. When my mother finally came stumbling out of the pub, it never even dawned on me to stop her driving us home because she'd been drinking. She whacked the radio up full blast and soon we were careering round narrow country lanes as Eric Burdon with his group The Animals blared out 'House of the Rising Sun'. Minutes later, we hit another car coming in the opposite direction. Luckily no one was hurt, but on the way home I remember thinking to myself: *If I'd been behind the wheel for real, then none of this would have happened. The sooner I learn how to drive the better.*

LITTLE LONE RANGE ROVER

I GUESS I MUST HAVE BEEN ABOUT SIX WHEN I STARTED TO look after myself at home. It suited me because I didn't like people offering to do stuff for me. It made me feel uncomfortable. Take going to school: I never knew exactly how or with whom I'd go of a morning so I'd often prefer just taking off on my own. My mum's hangovers regularly prevented her driving me. And while my dad was sometimes around to walk with me to the street corner, where he then peeled off towards the tube station, that wasn't a daily occurrence by any means. So more often than not I made my own way along the hectic London streets. The only really busy thoroughfare I had to cross was the Earls Court Road, right next to the police station. For some weird reason, I felt I'd be less likely to get run over in front of the local nick.

But not surprisingly, I was inches from death on numerous occasions. One time I actually got hit by a Bristol 405 just a few feet from the police station, but luckily I only got a few bruises and the driver didn't even stop. Hit 'n' runs were all the fashion back in those days. There wasn't much sympathy for a young kid out on his own. No one ever stopped me in the street to ask why my parents weren't around. I just got an almighty bollocking from that Bristol driver, who swore at me as he drove away, leaving me clutching my leg in the gutter. I hobbled off to school, trying hard to avoid the prying eyes of the nearby pedestrians who witnessed the entire 'accident' but did nothing to help me.

I really was on my own.

SINISTER MEN IN A SHOOTING BRAKE

LIFE AT HOME IN THAT HUGE, DRAUGHTY HOUSE CENTRED MAINLY around my mother and the tenants who shared the top floor with me. I was a light sleeper at the best of times so I'd often spend hours at night sitting at the window, writing down all the names and numbers of the cars passing in our street below.

I'd hear the tenants coming in and out of their rooms, even the sound of them on the toilet. I was surrounded by them, and although it disturbed me in some ways, as I've mentioned, it did reassure and make me feel safer in other ways.

One evening I was sitting on the boiling-hot radiator in front of my window, bobbing up and down when it got too hot and noting the details of all the cars whizzing by. I always tried to make sure I got the details of all the cars, even if they were travelling really fast and there was a whole pack of them.

Anyway. That particular night, I noticed that an Austin shooting brake kept driving very slowly around and around, stopping occasionally outside various houses in our street. Each time two men in black suits would get out, walk up the pathway to a house and knock on a door and wait for an answer, although hardly anyone opened their door to them. What on earth were they up to?

I watched these suspicious characters getting in and out of their Austin shooting brake for ages, when it finally dawned on me that they'd be passing our house pretty soon and maybe they'd try and lure us out, like they had with all the other neighbours.

So I rushed downstairs to the kitchen to look for my mother, but the lights were out and she was nowhere to be seen. I ran across the hall to the sitting room, but that was also pitch black, and then I started to panic. Although my mother often left me alone in the house, she usually told me when she was going out.

I was getting really worried about those men in the shooting brake. I was sure they'd be rolling up outside the house at any moment. Then I noticed a rustling behind the curtains in the front bay window of the sitting room. It really scared me and I stood frozen to the spot for a moment, wondering whether to kick out at the shape behind the curtains or just run for my life.

Just then my mother slid silently out from behind them and grabbed me by the arm. 'Ssssssh. They're coming.' I let out a big, irritated sigh because I presumed she was on the tranquillisers and booze. But before I had time to go into a sulk and retreat back up to my bedroom, I heard a pair of shoes climbing the steps just outside that same bay window.

'Shhhhhhh.' My mother gesticulated with her finger for me to stay quiet. I clutched her hand and we stood there, barely moving an inch as two voices came from outside.

'They must be in,' said one of the men. 'I can see some lights on at the top of the house.'

Who were these strange men and why were they knocking on our door? Were they burglars trying every house in our street until they found the perfect place to raid? I was shaking like a leaf by this time and very grateful to have my mother by my side for a change. She seemed remarkably calm about it all, which kind of reassured me.

Suddenly there was a very hard knock on the door. So loud it made me jump.

One of the men in suits then said: 'Bloody typical. The richer they are, the more they hide.'

Now I was convinced they were criminals and I was really angsting that they might knock the front door down and kill us both. My mother, still remarkably calm, looked down at me and implored me to be quiet by keeping her forefinger pressed hard to her lips. Yet despite all this drama, she still looked as if she didn't have a care in the world.

The men in black suits knocked again. This time it was an even harder, more aggressive knock. I presumed they were checking to see for certain if anyone was around, before they broke down the door.

'Better come back here tomorrow in the day, George. Maybe there's a lady of the house.'

Why would two killer burglars suddenly give up like that? It didn't make any sense whatsoever.

Now I was convinced my mother would be in mortal danger if she was at home tomorrow when I was at school. I'd have to skip school to be here to protect her. I looked up at her and noticed she'd lit a cigarette, which seemed a bit of a strange thing to do when two criminals were trying to break into our house.

Then I heard them turn around and begin walking down the steps away from the front door. It seemed that the imminent danger had now passed.

My mother continued to seem totally nonplussed by the entire frightening episode, although she did hold my hand for a couple of minutes and refused to let me move. Then, after a bit, she slipped behind the curtain once more to check out where the criminals had gone. I stood alongside her – still holding her hand – and glanced out of the window, too, and saw the Austin shooting brake drive off. It was only then I noticed it had the strangest aerial on it.

My mother let go of my hand and then flicked on the sitting-room light switch. I followed her across the hall and into the kitchen.

Then we both stopped in our tracks once again as we heard the unmistakable sound of a key struggling to find its way into the lock of the front door. Bloody hell. Had they come back to get us?

That key seemed to take ages to turn, which convinced me it might well be them trying to pick the front-door lock. I took a big gulp and grabbed my mother's hand again, ready to drag her up the stairs to escape the criminals.

CAR TROUBLE

Then the front door flew open to reveal my father, stumbling in after one of his classic Fleet Street liquid lunches. He was grinning from ear to ear and seemed very pleased with himself. I was so relieved to see him.

My mother greeted him with a peck on the cheek and then said very coolly: 'You just missed the TV-licence inspectors.' She smiled down at me and laughed. 'But we managed to give them the slip, didn't we?'

It was probably the only time in my entire childhood when a car had scared the life out of me.

GIVING WAY TO TRAFFIC

EVERYONE'S CHILDHOOD HAS ITS PIVOTAL MOMENTS, BUT looking back, it seems that mine had more than its fair share, good and bad. I remember one afternoon being reduced to tears when my mother managed to drop my prized Mercedes 300SL 'Gullwing' Coupe die-cast metal toy car down the steps at the front of the house.

She'd been showing some writer friend of my father's how the car's doors flipped upwards (hence the 'Gullwing' label) when it slipped out of her hand and bounced down the black-and-white tiled steps to eventually end up in three or four pieces on the walkway into our house. The most disturbing thing was that I knew she'd drop it the moment she drunkenly asked me to let her show her new 'friend' the car.

I looked up from the bottom of the steps with it in pieces to see if she was in any way concerned about what she'd just done. But she was already heading through the front door into the house to refill her glass with booze so that sort of said it all. My father's mate didn't seem that interested, either, but then most of the adults saw me as some slightly eccentric loner child who was allowed to mingle with them just because I didn't have any brothers or sisters to play with.

I tried desperately to fix the remains of my prized toy Mercedes back together, but it was hopeless. So I scooped the pieces up and ran past three adults and straight up the stairs to my safe little bedroom amongst the sitting tenants, well away from the noisy, drunken adults downstairs.

Typically, my mother managed to look guilt-ridden the next morning when I brought the four pieces of my prized Gullwing down for breakfast and laid them on the table in front of her in complete silence. She didn't say anything, but she did look straight at me with a bit of a pathetic look on her face, those gapped front teeth just visible.

I sat down in a strop with a bowl of Frosties and a glass of milk, determined to ignore her. It was all part of the game we played. I suppose I rather liked the feeling of holding something over her. Making her feel guilty was like a currency for me. It meant I could expect something in return.

Ten minutes later she squeezed her long, thin fingers into her favourite brown-suede-and-beige-crocheted driving gloves and announced we were going out. I grabbed my toy steering wheel off the marble table in the hall and began licking the suction thingy before we'd even got in the car. By the time she pressed the starter button on the Zodiac and it roared into life, I was in position to co-drive.

'Is it clear?' my mother mumbled to me.

She liked giving me the responsibility to see if there was any traffic coming before she shot out of the carport straight into our busy one-way road. I relished my role as navigator, but looking back on it, she was taking a huge risk allowing a seven-year-old kid to be her ears and eyes.

'Go!' I shouted when the coast seemed clear. We only had a few seconds because there was a big curve in our street, which meant you could only see the traffic for the final 100 yards or so. There were no traffic cameras back in those days so the cars came rushing down the road at speeds of up to 60 mph, making a serious crash more than just a possibility.

Sometimes my mum would hesitate and I'd have to say 'Go!' again just to get through to her. I reckon the tranquillisers slowed down her reactions, which didn't help.

But on this particular occasion she slammed her foot down on the accelerator, and the Zodiac dipped down into the gutter off the pavement at an alarming angle and then up again as we mounted the road itself and swerved in front of the traffic zooming just behind us. Two out of every three times we pulled out, someone would hoot and curse at my mother's apparently reckless driving. Typically, she ignored them all.

One time I remember a man road-raging us after she swerved out of the carport, cut him right up and then carried on as if it was all perfectly normal. We got to the traffic lights at the end of our road, and this man jumped out of his car in a fury and stomped towards us. My mum calmly locked all the doors and wound up her window. By the time he got to us, it was as if we were in this impregnable Zodiac fortress that no one could invade. My mother just smiled angelically as the man smashed his fist on the windscreen. Eventually he just gave up. We drove off as if nothing had happened and the incident was never, ever mentioned again.

ALFA MALE IN WINKLE-PICKERS

THE APPEARANCE OF RARE MAKES OF CARS PARKED IN OUR road always stuck in my mind because I was so obsessed with knowing more about them. One day I was out careering up and down the pavement in my silly little Noddy replica car with pedals when a very neat-looking red Alfa Romeo Spider parked up near our house. I examined it closely as a spivvy-looking chap with a pencil moustache climbed out, brushed down his suit and then cursed out loud when he trod in a pile of dog shit. That's when I noticed his winkle-pickers, which he seemed to have virtually sharpened to a point, except a smudge of dog shit now ruined the effect.

He looked sort of foreign, maybe Italian, to me, even though I didn't really know what an Italian looked like. I guess it was the make of car that made me think he was Italian because I'd instantly recognised the Alfa badge on the bonnet. It was the same with American cars in London. I always presumed they were all driven by Yanks. One time I was out with my dad when I met a notorious London gangster called Jack Spot in his Cadillac. He'd recently done an article with my father's paper. Spot had on a fedora hat and a double-breasted suit, complete with pointy shoes that all helped make him look very flash. I was stunned when he turned out not to have an American accent.

Anyway. Back to that Alfa Spider being driven by that spivvy-looking Italian geezer. He chucked me a sixpence and asked me to keep an eye on his car as he strolled past me near our house. I gave him the slightest nod of the head. The guy seemed to know I'd say yes before I'd even said it.

Then to my astonishment he skipped up the steps to my house and knocked on the door. I presumed he was there to see my mother. Nothing would surprise me when it came to her. No one answered the door at first, and then I remembered that my mother was out anyway.

I was about to tell him that when the front door opened, and it was the Frenchwoman teacher standing there in a very silky-looking dressing gown. She opened the door just wide enough for him to squeeze past her. They giggled and the front door slammed shut. I was glad I was staying out to watch his bloody car anyway, rather than listen to all the noise they'd no doubt make in her bedroom, which was next to mine.

I turned round and had another look at the Alfa Spider. It was a real beauty in bright red. Much sleeker lines than most of the boring old British sports cars that dominated the roads of London back then.

The Italian Stallion had zipped a black-leather cover over the top of the convertible Alfa's front seats, which also moulded perfectly over the steering wheel. I moved alongside the car to check it out. Then I looked around sneakily to see if he had reappeared, even though I knew he wouldn't be back for ages. The street was empty and only a handful of cars were driving past. Why would anyone pay attention to a little kid with a bad pudding-bowl haircut sitting in a silly-looking toy car?

Just then a black Zephyr police car with alarm bells shrilling and blue lights flashing approached on our road. I stepped away from the Alfa, convinced they might stop and arrest me for loitering with intent. But they clearly had other things on their mind and sped past.

It took another five minutes for me to pluck up the courage to get closer to the Alfa once again. This time I quickly leaned across and unzipped the section of the cover across the driver's seat, looked around one last time and clambered in.

I checked yet again to see if the coast was clear and tried to find the starter. I pressed it and, of course, nothing happened because the ignition key was in the Italian Stallion's trouser pocket, which was no doubt draped over a chair in the French teacher's little bedsit, where they both made all those weird noises. I grabbed the steering wheel with both hands and found it was covered in the softest leather I had ever felt in my short life. It made it so much easier to grip the wheel.

My feet touched something on the floor of the car. I took my hands off the steering wheel and scrabbled around to see what it was. Turned out to be a pair of goggles that the Italian Stallion must have used when he was out with hood down on a blustery day.

I adjusted the strap and put them on and sat there for a few moments, getting the hang of wearing these enormous goggles. I tried the starter button again. This time the engine roared into life and I sat there pressing my foot on the accelerator, revving and revving it up, much to the annoyance of various pedestrians.

Well, actually, it was my voice making all the noise but I was pretty good at impersonating a car engine so I kept up the pretence and drifted into my favourite car-driving mode. I was soon up there on cloud nine, swinging the steering wheel from side to side, yanking the gear stick forward and backward as I imagined myself driving up a steep hill and then down the other side. It was as if I had a movie screen stuck to the windscreen that showed the road ahead as it speeded towards me so that I could negotiate all the right moves.

I was soon engrossed in my own little motoring netherworld, making all the right car sounds and having a ball, in my head at least. Not surprisingly, I lost all track of time and even the noise of the real-life cars racing past became an irrelevance.

So I didn't notice a hand grabbing me by the scruff of my neck until it was too late. The hand pulled me out of the Alfa so roughly that I scratched the backs of my legs on the car door.

Of course it was Mr Spivvy, the Italian Stallion, and he was outraged that I had invaded his beloved car. I was then unceremoniously dumped in the gutter, while he inspected his car to make sure I had not damaged it. He eventually drove off with a spin of his tyres and a backwash of mud and slime. But I didn't care. In my head, I'd got to 'drive' a dream car, one that most people had not even heard of. It was well worth a few scratches and bruises.

So I brushed off some of the mud and trooped back up the steps towards my front door. I took a long, deep breath and then composed myself to try to explain the state of my clothes to my parents. I opened the door carefully and quietly in the hope they would not hear me and slipped silently into the hallway. My mother shouted out from the kitchen, 'Is that you?' I pondered for a moment on how to respond. Then I decided to say nothing because I knew my mother wouldn't bother coming out into the hall in case it was one of her tenants. I slipped ever so quietly up the stairs towards the tenants' quarters and my little bedroom. By the time my mother stumbled into the hallway, I'd gone into the bathroom I shared with the tenants for a wash and brush up.

WAITING FOR A TAXI

But it never comes.
Taxxiiiiiiiiiiiii.

'Waiting For Your Taxi',
Ian Dury and The Blockheads

RIGHT FROM AN EARLY AGE I'D ALWAYS BEEN A VERY NERVOUS passenger in cars. I studied drivers' skills so closely. I was quick to work out if someone was either a good or a bad driver, and as a result I had some very scary journeys, during which I'd get very stressed.

What always surprised me was the way that both my mother and father seemed so relaxed when they were being driven by other people. Yet there I was, a little kid getting myself twisted up in knots if a driver cut a corner or didn't brake early enough. And let's face it, there are many of them out there.

But a lot of my most deep-set fears were sparked by an incident that remains now as vivid in my memory as the day it happened, when I was six or seven years old. My mum had taken me on one of her magical mystery tours to meet a 'friend' in a pub out in the countryside somewhere. I guess it was Sussex, but none of that matters because it was the aftermath that has lodged itself so indelibly in my mind.

CAR TROUBLE

I was sitting in the Zodiac in the pub car park, sucking on the straw of a bottle of lemonade and dipping in and out of a packet of crisps, while doing my favourite impersonation of Stirling Moss.

I didn't mind being left out there for hours so long as I was in my motoring netherworld. I also didn't care who was watching me because I was immersed in my own little world to the exclusion of everyone else. I'd sit there with a steely look of determination in my eyes, swinging the steering wheel back and forth, round and round, happy to be able to indulge myself in my seemingly never-ending daydreaming fantasies.

When my mother finally emerged from the pub, I didn't even think twice about the way she was weaving towards the Zodiac. True, I hadn't been too keen on her drinking and driving since she'd had that prang, but at least I was out and about in the car, which was more important than anything else.

One of the good things about having an eccentric mother who liked a drink and downed a lot of tranquillisers was that she *never* made me feel uncomfortable about my own weirdness. So when she clambered into the Zodiac and said very casually 'move over', it sounded as normal as talking about the weather. I was almost tempted there and then to flick on the ignition and drive her home.

But instead I slid across the bench seat, delighted that she hadn't told me to go in the back. I loved it up front, and often she'd let me be in charge of all the switches, ranging from the lights to the radio, which I would be allowed to twiddle with until we had a good pop-music station blaring along as we drove.

But she hadn't even started the engine yet that day, so I sat back and waited patiently for the V6 to burst into life. Initially my mother struggled a bit to even get the key into the ignition, but there was nothing new about that so I watched without comment. I didn't feel I had the right to point out when she was tipsy. In any case, what difference would it make? We weren't likely to get out of the car and get a bus home.

With the key now firmly in the ignition, she tried to start the engine but nothing happened. This wasn't so unusual because cars back in those days often took a few attempts to fire up. I remained quiet, but my eyes were locked on the ignition because there wasn't a single spark coming from the engine. Not good.

Five minutes later and we were still nowhere nearer starting the Zodiac. My mother peeled off her brown-suede-and-beige-crocheted driving gloves and hit the steering wheel in frustration with the palms of her hand. But she didn't say a word. I guess that was about the nearest I ever saw her get to losing her temper. As for swearing, she might have liked a drink, but she came from the generation where the 'f' word was rarely uttered, and *never* by a lady.

A thin, balding, middle-aged man wandered up to us. He was smiling broadly. 'Need a hand?' My mother was never one to turn down a free offer, so she charmingly engaged the man, even though my instinct told me immediately not to trust him an inch. I'd always had this over-sensitive radar inside me from an early age. Usually, I started any contact with other people from a position of complete and utter suspicion. That way I wouldn't be disappointed. They'd have to win me over before I'd trust them, and this Good Samaritan seemed odd to me. He must have spotted me scowling at him because he patted me condescendingly on the head when I got out of the Zodiac with my mother. I ignored him, naturally.

The stranger quickly popped up the hood and started fiddling around with the engine. Every now and again my mother would try and start the Zodiac under his instructions, but the engine was dead, except for a sizzling sound, which her new best friend eventually announced must have been the distributor.

I'd watched him closely throughout and concluded that he was putting on a bit of a performance for us, which made me trust him even less. However, my mother didn't seem in the least bit concerned by him, although she never seemed to worry about stuff like that.

'Where you off to, then?' asked the bald, greasy, middle-aged man.

When my mother explained where we lived, a huge smile broke out on the man's face.

'Small world. I'm taking my cab down that way for work. I'll give you a ride . . . no trouble.'

I didn't like the way he said 'trouble', but then what did I know: a young kid.

CAR TROUBLE

As he said the word 'cab', our knight in shining nylon had nodded towards an old black London cab parked up in the pub car park near us. I was completely thrown because I'd got it in my head that black cabs were only ever driven for work so what was he doing in it 'off duty'? Then I thought about what he'd just said and I supposed it made vague sense, and in any case, how else were we going to get home that day?

So we locked up the Zodiac and walked across the car park towards the black cab. It wasn't so bad, really. I quite fancied the idea of a relatively long-distance ride in a cab, as I hadn't been in many in my short life.

As we were about to get in, the 'cabbie' became much more chummy with my mother, and I noticed him pat her on the arse as he opened the front passenger door. I didn't like that one bit, and it sparked a big surge of protectiveness inside me because I hated it when men did anything like that to my mother. I took a deep breath to stop myself kicking him in the shin because I knew my mother would be annoyed with me if I ruined our chances of a free lift all the way home.

Looking back on it, I should have been thinking about other aspects of the cab at that moment, but that incident had distracted me from studying his tatty-looking vehicle and had focused my attention on disliking him. It was only after we'd set off and I was in the back of the cab on my own with my mother settled alongside the cabbie up front that I began to get a really bad feeling about what was happening.

I might not have been in many cabs during my childhood, but I realised that the front passenger seat in a black London taxi didn't usually have any seats because it was where the luggage was put. So how come my mum was clearly sitting on a passenger seat next to the cabbie? What was going on? At that moment I heard the cabbie mumble something about 'nice legs', and as I leaned forward I noticed his left hand on my mother's knee. He saw me watching him and slid the glass partition closed so it was much harder to hear what they were saying. Then he turned up the radio so loud I could barely hear anything apart from Cilla Black bawling away about 'Anyone Who Had a Heart', which I hated.

I looked across at the speedometer, as I often did, and we were already doing at least 50 and the cab was picking up more speed very quickly. As it swung around one sharp corner, I fell across the back seat and hit my head on the door handle. That's when I caught a glance from my mum. She did not look happy, but I didn't know what to do.

The cabbie pulled something out from under the right side of his seat. It was a three-quarters-empty bottle of Scotch. As he took a long swig, we swerved precariously. Then he tried to push the bottle into my mother's lap.

I very quietly slid the glass partition open slightly without him noticing and just heard him say: 'Have a drink, darlin'. It's good for you.'

It was the first time in my life I ever saw my mother turn down a whisky. She was looking straight ahead now, and although she wasn't showing any fear in her expression, I knew she must be worried. I had to do something.

We swung around a roundabout at about 60 and onto a dual carriageway, which was disastrous for us because it meant there were no crossroads or traffic lights to stop at where we could jump out. On the dual carriageway, the cabbie stamped down hard on the accelerator and the speedometer soon said 75 mph and the needle was still creeping upwards. We were completely trapped in the taxi, except it wasn't really a taxi at all.

The cabbie demolished the rest of his bottle of whisky and merrily chucked it out of the window as we hit 90 mph. The bottle smashed into little pieces on a barrier. I know because I turned and watched as he threw it.

I was sitting on the fold-down seat that backed onto the barrier between the passengers' and the driver's area now. I was up against the glass partition, which was still slightly cracked open so I could hear what he was saying.

Then he started singing along with Engelbert Humperdinck's 'Please Release Me'. The words simply added to the surreal, terrifying atmosphere in the cab as we charged nearer and nearer to 100 mph on that dual carriageway. I sneaked another look at my mother, who was staring ahead with one of her familiar stoic expressions on her face. But I think she must have been feeling responsible for all this. Then the cabbie grabbed her knee again, before trying to run his hand further up her leg.

I was so angry. I shouted through the small gap in the glass partition: 'Leave my mother alone!'

The cabbie turned and grinned, and I noticed him defiantly squeeze my mother's thigh tightly. I flipped and tried to rip open the glass partition while we were travelling at more than 90 mph.

He pushed me away while still holding the steering wheel with one hand. We swerved across into the slow lane and narrowly missed a lorry alongside us, whose driver blew his horn at us with anger.

My mother, the person who always kept herself calm to the point of being impersonal and appearing cold, was still looking straight ahead of her. She seemed virtually frozen to the spot.

I looked through the windscreen, and thank goodness we seemed to be coming to the end of the dual carriageway and he would have to slow down a bit. In a weird way, my mother's refusal to lash out at him had helped to momentarily calm things because we both knew there was nothing we could do until the cab slowed down enough for us to escape.

Meanwhile, the cabbie began singing again at the top of his voice. I can't actually remember who this time. I convinced myself he believed he'd captured us and was going to take us somewhere and lock us up and then do horrible things to my mother and me. It all felt doomed. I couldn't see us escaping. I imagined all these awful things happening to us so vividly that they started to turn real in my head.

We eventually slowed down to about 60 mph in a built-up area, but there still hadn't been any traffic lights or crossroads to stop our nightmare journey, and the atmosphere in the cab was muted, despite his never-ending out-of-tune singing.

But my mother still hadn't uttered a word and I started to sense that it was really frustrating our cabbie/kidnapper that she was not responding. He began looking across at her with a quizzical look on his face rather than licking his lips like earlier. But then my mother could be confusing at the best of times.

While he was being distracted by my mother, I tried the door handle so I'd be ready to jump out when we slowed right down, but it was locked and my attempt to fiddle with it caused a clicking noise, which alerted the cabbie to what I was doing.

'Don't worry. You'll be home soon.'

Then he laughed to himself in a deranged way. My mother still didn't take her eyes off the road ahead.

I was now so scared I couldn't even cry. It felt like we were trapped in a nightmare, but at least my mother was there, although she was hardly capable of rescuing me. Although we were in this together so that made it slightly easier to handle.

And the singing cabbie was, well, still singing.

I tried to make myself angry in the hope it might help me snap out of my self-induced gloom about our prospects. How the hell could he have the nerve to do this to us? It was outrageous. This strange nagging feeling of wanting to take revenge on him started to eat into me. I hated the way he was now controlling our destiny.

Yet in the middle of all this, I also begrudgingly conceded to myself that he wasn't a bad driver. Here he was, smashed out of his head on a bottle of Scotch, and yet he was still quite capable behind the wheel. In some ways that frightened me even more because it meant he would be more difficult to trick if and when we got a chance to escape.

At that moment the cabbie used his left hand to bang the glass partition closed again. I think he knew my mother would never leave me in the back of that cab so in effect we were both trapped, even though she could have got out of her door any time the cab slowed right down. My heart sank because it meant that even if we did stop at traffic lights or a crossroads, it still would be virtually impossible to get out of the cab.

I needed a plan. My life so far had been filled with internal plans because I'd spent so much time on my own. I was always walking up the street thinking about what I'd do if a lorry suddenly mounted the pavement and came careering towards me or how I'd react if the TV-licensing men came back. Planning how to deal with hypothetical situations was part of my character.

CAR TROUBLE

But this time a real plan was needed that would help save our lives. That might sound dramatic, but that's how it felt in the back of that cab that day. I still had visions of being locked in a dark, damp cellar with that horrible man standing over us.

I decided to sit back in the rear seat and let the cabbie think I had given up the fight after he'd slammed that glass partition closed. I looked around me for any loose objects and then spotted the ashtray that was attached to the inside of the door panel.

I looked at my mother and the cabbie, and neither of them even glanced behind at me, so I grabbed the metal ashtray and twisted it. It easily came off its hinges into my hand. It was quite big and deep and it was shaped like a small curved cup, so I could dig my fingers into it, which made it into a metallic knuckleduster, in a sense.

In the middle of all this I kept a close watch on the cabbie's eyes in the rear-view mirror. He didn't seem interested in me, thank goodness, although I didn't like the look of the bloodshot whites of his eyes one bit.

We were now driving through the south London suburbs and he had no choice but to slow the cab down to about 40 mph. I scrambled across the floor of the cab from the back seat to the partition, right behind the cabbie's head, so he couldn't see me, and then I tried to get my mother's attention.

At first she didn't even notice me. I crouched there for what seemed like ages in the hope she might spot me out of the corner of her eye. Every time he took a corner at speed I'd struggle to maintain my balance, but luckily he never once looked in his rear-view mirror.

Eventually my mother turned her head ever so slightly to her right and our eyes locked on each other for a moment. I opened my hands in an expression of expectation. In other words, 'What do we do now?'

Of course, she must have felt trapped because she knew the doors in the back of the cab were locked internally so I couldn't get out. I gestured with my thumbs up as if to say, 'We have to do something and do you agree?' She nodded ever so slightly in case he noticed, although I didn't really know if she had a clue what I was on about.

Within a minute or so, the cab slowed right down for our first set of traffic lights. I tensed my fist with that ashtray around it and waited until we'd almost come to a complete stop.

'Now don't be thinking you can just nip out here,' said the cabbie in a flat, empty monotone.

The lights turned green and he surged ahead so fast that there was no way I could have activated any plan. I sat back in the rear seat and let out a huge huff of irritation and frustration. This was not looking good at all.

Just then the cabbie slammed on the brakes when a couple of young kids skipped across a pedestrian crossing in front of us. 'Fuckin' hell,' he yelled in irritation. I watched the two kids charge across the road and knew they would be so quick we wouldn't have a chance.

My heart sank again, but then I looked up and noticed that an old lady was about to walk onto the zebra crossing, which would hold up the cab for much longer because she was walking very slowly. Right. It was time. Now or never.

I smashed that ashtray as hard as I could through the partition between us, and by some miracle I didn't get cut as the glass shattered into little fragments. I held my hands and arms over my head and scrambled through the partition. My mother had already swung open the door and we virtually fell out onto the road.

The cabbie tried to make a grab for me, but then he noticed the lollipop lady looking straight at him with a quizzical look on her face. We brushed ourselves down and went straight into the nearest shop, knowing full well that he would never stop the cab and come after us in such an exposed place.

I turned and watched him smashing the steering wheel of the cab over and over and over again with frustration as he drove off. I tried to memorise the number plate, but I knew from the look on my mother's face that she wasn't going to take this any further. We were safe and well after a weird experience, but she knew perfectly well that the police would never chase it up.

The following day the AA towed the Zodiac to a garage near that pub and it was repaired. As usual, my mother and I never mentioned that disturbing day ever again. I think she was reluctant to admit where she'd been to my father and I knew instinctively not to open my mouth. As ever, the responsibility was on me to protect her. I liked the feeling that gave me.

CAPTAIN CONRAD AND HIS WHISKY/MILK

MY FATHER HAD THIS OLD FRIEND – ANOTHER WRITER – FROM THE Spanish Civil War who now lived in Steyning, near Brighton, on the south coast. His name was Conrad Phillips and, like so many of my parents' friends, he was completely potty. Conrad had lived with his second wife in a haze of whisky and milk (his favourite drink) for many years, and the highlight of their month was when my father and mother visited them at their very creepy Gothic-style mansion in Steyning, which I vividly recall had a horrible fold-out wooden bed in the hall where I used to have to sleep whenever we stayed.

Conrad Phillips had this huge mane of thick, yellowing grey hair that made him look very much like a fading matinee idol tinged with an overdose of nicotine. Conrad had this remarkable ability to talk to me on my own level, even though I was a child. He didn't speak down to me. He treated me as an equal, and in turn I adored him because he always had a mischievous grin on his face.

But when I look back on my childhood memories of Conrad Phillips, there is one particular road trip that I will never forget. We'd all trooped down to his house one weekend, and he'd decided that instead of staying in and drinking themselves stupid, we'd actually go onto the Sussex Downs and have a day out. The only problem was that Conrad insisted on driving and he had recently suffered an appalling stroke, which meant his left leg was in a calliper and his left arm was completely frozen and, in his words, 'bloody useless'.

Now you might wonder how anyone with half their body malfunctioning could even contemplate driving any car, let alone a tank – otherwise known as Conrad's Wolseley 6/110. But Conrad wasn't the type of character to let a few disabilities get in the way of his driving. The blue Wolseley was automatic and he'd put a small lever on the steering wheel so he could turn it with one hand. It wasn't exactly ingenious, but he claimed it meant he could drive perfectly well. Conrad noisily and indignantly had turned down all offers of a ride in our Zodiac up to the Downs, so we all clambered into the Wolseley with some trepidation.

After all, if Conrad had been alive today he would have been taken off the road and banned for life for even attempting to drive with those sorts of medical problems. But Conrad did do one very sensible thing before we set off: he made sure my parents were well and truly sloshed so they wouldn't notice any of his unusual driving habits, or so he hoped.

I was allowed to stick my plastic steering wheel complete with column gear change on the back of the Wolseley's blue-leather front-bench seats. I was delighted because it might stop me getting nervous once we set off.

But it was hard not to notice Conrad's ailments as he hopped and shuffled across the gravel of his driveway to get into the Wolseley. The poor bloke was dragging his foot more than Ian Dury on acid and his arm hung down like a limp piece of white cod.

In the back seat, I dutifully pretended to be driving with my fake plastic steering wheel before he'd even started the Wolseley up. Conrad and I had talked many times about cars and which ones I liked the best so he knew perfectly well that I had a pair of very beady eyes when it came to driving.

In fact, just before he leaned forward with his one good hand to start the engine, he looked behind and gave me the most enormous wink, which neither of my sloshed parents even noticed. I liked that.

It meant we had something going on between us and that always made me feel more grown up. I went back to driving my plastic toy steering wheel, but out of the corner of my eye I was watching Conrad like a hawk.

I was fascinated by how he could manage to drive the car with only one leg and one hand functioning. I did have complete trust in his abilities, though, because he was one of those sorts of characters you felt safe with. He'd never give up and he'd get you there, even if it cost him his life.

But even I was a bit startled by what happened next. He struggled to push the column change automatic gear lever into 'D' for Drive with one hand and then we moved off very slowly for a moment. Then Conrad slammed his boot down on the accelerator and we shot into the path of an oncoming lorry. It was only when Conrad struggled to lift his head to get a view of what was ahead that I realised he was also paralysed in the neck.

Anyway. We managed to avoid the lorry by inches and I looked over at my father, who was sweating profusely and looking very nervous. The drink had definitely worn off, although my mother was, as ever, as cool as ice. Nothing could break that calm demeanour.

The journey through the back streets of Brighton and Hove until we got up onto the main road across the Downs should have been terrifying, but it was difficult to be scared when Conrad kept winking at me. Also, I didn't want him to see me looking worried because then I would have felt I had let him down. Silly, but true.

As we progressed, I became increasingly fascinated by that strange-looking knob on the steering wheel that enabled Conrad to manoeuvre the car. Without it, he would not have been able to steer at all. I reckon it actually helped Conrad to steer even more accurately than if he hadn't had any medical problems in the first place. When he reversed into a parking space at our first port of call, a pub, he managed to squeeze into a tiny, narrow space in a way my mum and her 'normal' steering would never have managed. So far, so good.

However, Conrad looked shattered when they all traipsed off to the pub, leaving me in the car as usual. It was clearly something he was determined to keep doing even though he wasn't really anywhere near fit enough to drive.

A few minutes later, my dad slipped out with the customary bottle of pop and a bag of Smith's crisps, containing a blue baggie of salt. He seemed quite stressed and grimaced rather than giving out his usual smile when he handed me the drink and crisps. I had a feeling that whatever was wrong, it was connected to Conrad.

But for the moment they were all happily ensconced back in the pub, so I clambered over the leather bench seats and plonked myself in the driver's seat and started examining that strange-looking knob that Conrad had attached to the steering wheel.

I immersed myself in my driving netherworld, as usual, and tried to imagine I was steering the Wolseley for real, but I used the same knob on the steering wheel as Conrad did rather than both hands and it made a change. The great thing about fantasy worlds, especially when you are a child, is that you can cut everything else out of your head while you're 'living', and I was doing just that in Conrad's Wolseley in that pub car park.

I guess it was about half an hour later, and I was imagining myself swerving the Wolseley around Brands Hatch, when there was a big knock on the window. It was Conrad and he looked very drunk and even redder in the face than usual.

'Move over, sunshine,' he said in a very jolly voice, which cleverly disguised his inebriated state. I was about to clamber back into the rear seat when he pulled me back. 'Hold on. Hold on.'

So I sat there in the slight dip in the bench seats. Conrad wasn't doing much, apart from struggling to keep his head from slumping on the steering wheel.

'Press the starter,' he mumbled.

I couldn't believe what was happening.

'Come on. You're going to help me.'

I didn't answer, but he knew I was up for it. So I pressed the black starter button and the Wolseley rumbled into life.

'Here,' he said, patting the seat right next to him. 'You can steer.'

I didn't question him in case he changed his mind, but sat so close to him that I could just reach the steering wheel as he let down the handbrake with his one good hand. We rolled forward, and his one good leg pressed downwards as he touched the accelerator with his shoe.

The Wolseley's bonnet rose up in front of me as Conrad pressed down harder and we shot across the car park and narrowly missed two couples who'd just walked out of the side entrance of the pub. I felt strangely empowered to be steering the car.

We swerved around the car park for about two or three minutes and then I noticed my mother, father and Conrad's wife, Pam, emerge from the pub exit. They looked horrified when they noticed me leaning across and helping to steer the car. Conrad then stopped the Wolseley and put it into 'P' for Park.

I moved aside because I presumed that was the end of my 'driving lesson', but Conrad said, 'Hang on. Hang on. I need your help, little man.'

I was aware that his wife and my mother and father were stumbling into the car, obviously pretty pissed after their session at the pub.

'Right,' said Conrad, turning to talk to his other passengers. 'This young man is going to help me drive home because my arm is killing me.'

I turned and looked into his face and bloodshot eyes for a few moments and considered my options. Here was a seventy-five-year-old stroke victim admitting his one good hand was in such bad condition that he needed me – a six-year-old child – to help steer his car back to his house, where my mother's car awaited us.

I didn't respond. I just thought I'd see if any of the adults present had any better suggestions. None of them uttered a word, so I shrugged my shoulders and nodded at Conrad and off we went.

It turned out not to be that scary at all and probably helped me understand the feel of a car and its steering more than anything else up to that time. At one stage, we stopped at some traffic lights and got a couple of odd glances. The closest shave came when we pulled into a garage for some petrol and there was a police car lining up ahead of us. Conrad nodded at me to slide away onto the bench seat next to him and they were none the wiser.

Alongside me, Conrad's very drunk wife sat slumped against the window, not saying a word. Later, when we stopped at one junction,

CAR TROUBLE

I looked behind me and both my parents were fast asleep, leaning up against each other. I still don't know if they ever even recalled the fact that I helped drive that Wolseley about ten miles home.

But that experience undoubtedly fuelled my obsession with driving real cars. It was yet another taste of what was to come, and I convinced myself it would all happen sooner rather than later.

That night, I had to sleep in that creepy hallway in the bed that came out of the wall. I hated being stuck there in the dark, even though I'd just done something potentially a lot scarier by co-piloting a Wolseley home on the streets of Sussex.

The following day, I felt very confident while watching my mother as she drove the Zodiac along the old Brighton-to-London A23 road. I had a real feel for the car now. I knew what it was like to turn corners and switch lanes on a dual carriageway. I understood the importance of turning and checking the blind spot alongside you just in case there was a car there. I also reckoned I'd completely grown out of that silly stick-on steering wheel.

GLAMOROUS GRANNIES & CHAUFFEUR ERIC

WHEN I WAS ABOUT SIX, MY PARENTS TOOK ME TO BUTLIN'S Holiday Camp in Bognor, in Sussex, where my father was helping to judge something called the 'Glamorous Grandmothers' competition for his newspaper, *Reveille*. My mother had suggested I come along with them, probably because she knew how boring it would be and therefore I might prove a handy diversion in case she was expected to talk to anyone she didn't know or like.

But the reason I remember that trip so clearly is down to one particular car. My dad's newspaper had laid on a chauffeur-driven Mercedes 280SE to take us down to Bognor. You might be wondering how I can be so sure about the make of car. Oh, that's easy. The Mercedes 280SE was my favourite car *of all time*. I adored the unique stacked headlights, not to mention the lines of the car, which were so smooth and sleek, even compared to some of the British classics such as Jags or Daimlers.

My parents happily agreed to let me sit up front in the silver Mercedes while they knocked back a few liveners from a flask and created their own cosy little alcohol-fuelled bubble in the back seat for the three-hour journey. To begin with, I sat shyly in complete silence alongside the chauffeur, who at first seemed a little irritated that some kid was sitting there in his 'space'.

I wasn't used to being driven on long car journeys with anyone apart from my mother. I liked the way the Mercedes' bonnet lifted every time the chauffeur accelerated. People in other cars looked at us a lot at traffic lights, and I felt quite smug about being out in such a 'flashy' car, being driven by a man in a black cap complete with a neat patent peak.

I was fascinated by his driving skills because they were different from anything I had ever seen before. We were only a few minutes into the journey when I noticed he was braking in a strange way at traffic lights and on junctions. He'd press his foot quite hard on the brake and then let it off for a split second just before we stopped. It was intriguing me so much that in the end I asked him why he was doing it. It was as if he didn't like the fact I'd spotted his very subtle technique. But then I asked him about why he timed his indicators so precisely, and this time he perked up and began explaining to me in intricate detail some of the tricks of his trade. His name turned out to be Eric, and he said he always braked that way because it made stopping the vehicle much smoother, which in turn ensured the passengers' comfort.

The very next time Eric braked at some traffic lights I watched him even more closely, and he was absolutely right. Instead of a jerky stopping motion, it was so smooth you hardly noticed the car coming to halt. Naturally, my half-sloshed parents in the back seat didn't notice any of this. For the following couple of hours I watched Eric's every move and made a note in my head to remember his 'tips' when I got behind the wheel for real.

When we finally got to Bognor in our silver Mercedes 280SE, my parents stumbled out of the back of the car to the entrance to Butlin's, which was closed to the public during the winter months but had been specially opened for *Reveille*'s 'Glamorous Grandmothers' contest. Back in those days, most grandmothers looked as if they really were . . . grandmothers. If the contest existed today it would be marshalled and owned by Simon Cowell.

God knows who won that year. I was more interested in when Eric would be driving us back to London in the 280SE.

MOST DEADLY DRIVE-BY IN THE WORLD

ON 22 NOVEMBER 1963, JFK WAS ASSASSINATED IN FRONT OF that grassy knoll in Dallas, Texas, by Lee Harvey Oswald. I only know the specific date because I Googled it for this book, obviously. But I do remember very clearly how I felt that day because I just happened to be watching our big cumbersome black-and-white telly on my own when the first dramatic newsflash came on the screen.

It showed grainy footage of JFK's sleek-looking black presidential limousine Lincoln SS-100-X with 'taxi' doors as the First Lady, Jackie, cradled her dying husband in her arms while the limo raced through the crowded streets towards a nearby medical centre. Naturally, I was more interested in that Lincoln than anything else. My eyes homed on it as I watched the telly.

That afternoon I'd been *vrooming* a dozen Dinky and Corgi cars in and out of a small-scale toy garage. I was only seven years old, but I was well used to being on my own at home. In fact, I rather liked it because I'd already started to develop an aversion to my parents' drinking, which made me prefer not to be with them in the house when they were 'on the bottle'.

CAR TROUBLE

I was so obsessed by the dead President's limo that the very next morning I raided my piggy bank and popped up the road to the toyshop to see if they stocked a Corgi version and ended up with one with a powder-blue paint job. Later that day on my bedroom floor I dramatically reconstructed the assassination – complete with gunshots and engine noises – with the Lincoln speeding off with the already almost dead President being tended to by his soon-to-be widow.

Lee Harvey Oswald was played by one of my tiny plastic-soldier snipers, and I found a couple of other little plastic figures to play the President and First Lady. I redesigned my toy garage and other toy buildings and set up my own version of the grassy knoll in Texas, complete with my brand-new powder-blue toy Lincoln convertible on the floor of my bedroom.

I replicated the sound of the rifle going off with a 'phoar' over and over again that day, and then I stopped everything for a few moments to find two more little plastic-model men to act as the Secret Service bodyguards. I even flicked a few tiny specks of ketchup on 'JFK', but the bit I most enjoyed was pushing the Lincoln around the floor as it careered round corners trying to get to the hospital in time to save the President's life.

I was on at least the fifth dramatic reconstruction of that last, desperate dash following the shooting when a shoe came crunching down on top of my toy Lincoln. I looked up and it was the boyfriend of the annoying Frenchwoman tenant who lived next to my bedroom. He rested his boot on the Lincoln without actually crushing it, in a very intimidating manner. He wanted me to stop making so much noise. I looked up at him, towering over me, and nodded my head, with absolutely no intention of quietening down. I was just irritated that this strange man had dared to cut right through the middle of my fantasy world and bring me crashing back into reality. I wished my mother would allow me to have a lock fitted on my bedroom door. I hated the lack of privacy that came with sleeping in a room hemmed in by strangers.

The moment my bedroom door closed behind him, I grabbed the Lincoln and wiped its roof clean of the horrible scuff marks from his boot. He hadn't actually damaged it, but it felt as if an enemy alien had just invaded my own special world. When I then heard giggling and moaning coming from the Frenchwoman's room, I simply turned up the volume of Oswald's rifle and added a lot of car-engine noises to drown them out.

Over the following couple of years I developed a morbid interest in the whole JFK shooting, although my main aim was to push that Lincoln round my bedroom floor at high speed. And I never proved beyond reasonable doubt that Lee Harvey Oswald really did kill JFK. But none of that mattered.

I was equally obsessed with the Great Train Robbery, which happened a couple of months before the JFK assassination. I created a train track and a bridge just like the one on which the train was stopped and raided in Buckinghamshire.

There were many moments in my childhood when my fantasy world came to the rescue of reality.

ROAD-TESTING ROGER'S NEW MOTOR

IT'S EARLY 1964 AND MY LOVE FOR TV'S *BONANZA* HAS BEEN replaced by *The Saint*, starring Roger Moore and that weird-looking Volvo P1800 Coupe he drives everywhere. There was something about the shape of it that captured my imagination and I hardly ever saw any of them around on the streets of London, which naturally made them even more intriguing. Corgi brought out a toy model version, which I liked playing with when I was lying on the floor in front of our big old telly in the sitting room watching schmoozer Roger greasing around in his tight-fitting pencil suit with a tie as narrow as an elastic band.

In the months after *The Saint* hit the small screen, I noted more of those same Volvo Coupes going past the house and I scribbled down their details with great enthusiasm. I guess sales of that model took off mainly because of the publicity from *The Saint*.

One weekend at that time I was wandering around the streets of my neighbourhood examining the speedometers of my favourite cars when I came across one of the very same Volvo Coupes. I pulled my toy version out of my pocket and spent what seemed like hours (more like minutes) comparing them both. I was always fascinated by just how accurately Corgi and other toymakers managed to replicate the real thing. The answer was not very. It was like a token effort, really, and I was usually very disappointed that my toy version wasn't more similar to 'the real thing'.

Anyway, that day I was studying the real Volvo Coupe's unusual door handle when I noticed the button was up, which meant it was unlocked. I paused for a few seconds, rubbed my chin and looked around in both directions. It didn't take long for me to summon up the courage to try and open the door. The street was still deserted.

I pressed down on the door handle and it fell open with ease. I checked in both directions again and slipped into the driver's seat. It was a small bucket seat, a much better fit than my mother's Zodiac bench seat.

I was terrified the owner might appear, but that fear was soon overcome as I immersed myself in a dose of fantasy driving. I flicked on a few switches and pretended to start up the car, which was obviously impossible because there was no key. But it was fun being in the Volvo because it was so different from any other car I had ever sat in.

I was carefully adjusting the rear-view mirror when I noticed a bobby coming towards me. He was a long way off so I knew he couldn't have spotted me – yet. I had a choice: either duck down very low and hope he didn't see me or get out of the car very quickly and walk – not run – in the opposite direction.

But even in the time it took me to think that through, he was getting closer so I had to make a quick decision. I took a deep breath and decided to make a run for it. I couldn't risk that copper stumbling upon me, because I had effectively broken into the Volvo.

I opened the door very slowly in the hope he wouldn't notice it and then slid out at a very low angle, virtually straight into the pavement. I scrambled off in the opposite direction, but resisted the temptation to run because I knew that would look far more suspicious.

Walking back at a steady rate towards the other end of the road, I didn't dare look back. I just kept my head straight ahead and hoped he hadn't spotted anything. Those few seconds seemed like minutes.

Suddenly, I heard a whistle go. It had to be that copper. I was petrified. Do I stop or just keep walking? He must have seen me and was now in pursuit. A vision of being locked up in jail flashed through my mind. Maybe I should make a run for it? But I knew that would only make him chase me harder so I just kept walking. I had no choice.

He let off a second blow of his whistle, and I could tell from the sound of it that he was much closer to me now. He must have been running in my direction. I felt the butterflies in my tummy fluttering so badly that I was starting to feel nauseous.

But I kept my head up and walked in a straight line. Maybe I could talk my way out of this? The frustrating thing was that I didn't dare turn round to see how close he was in case he caught my eye, and then he'd know I'd been up to no good.

I then turned the corner and bumped straight into my father walking in my direction. It completely threw me, and for a split second when I looked up at him I didn't know what to say. I must have panicked, but he was so pleased to see me that I don't think he noticed the state I was in. Instead he beamed with delight and I let out a forced smile.

'Where are you off to in such a hurry?' he asked.

I just shrugged my shoulders and smiled up at him again. He must have been going down to the off-licence, I suppose.

But at least bumping into my dad meant I had an excuse to turn around and see where my police pursuer was. I was relieved my dad was there because then maybe I'd get off with a warning rather than being frogmarched down to the local police station.

The young copper bounded up to us, and I virtually put my hands out so he could cuff me there and then, but there was a big smile on his face, which seemed odd.

'You just dropped this on the street,' said the bobby. It was my Volvo Coupe Corgi model.

I was completely lost for words, but forced a smile.

'Hey,' said my father. 'Thank the nice officer.'

I looked up at the policeman, took a big gulp and muttered, 'Thanks.'

CAR TROUBLE

That incident should have been a big lesson and a warning never to steal cars in real life. The trouble with being in any car was that it just made me want to drive even more.

THOSE MAGNIFICENT MEN IN
THEIR DRIVING MACHINES

OBVIOUSLY MANY OF MY CHILDHOOD EXPERIENCES WITH CARS were connected to my mother's insatiable appetite for breaking up the tedium of her life. My mother and her two sisters were all on the books of a theatrical agent for minor acting roles. Most of the time that meant working as extras on movies, although occasionally they got walk-on parts, and I remember overhearing my mother telling my father how one of my spinster aunts had been asked out on a date by a well-known British Hollywood matinee idol when she was working at Shepperton film studios.

Undeniably one of my mother's main aims with all these activities was to avoid dealing with the rocky aspects of her relationship with my father. From my perspective, I'd always prefer skipping school and going on a film set, so I was game to join them.

In late 1964, my mother and aunts got 'called up' to work as extras at an airfield in Kent on a Hollywood film called *Those Magnificent Men in Their Flying Machines*, starring Stuart Whitman, Sarah Miles, Terry-Thomas and James Fox.

The morning was spent being immersed in a crowd of people who were supposed to be 'waving off' the aeroplanes as they took off for

CAR TROUBLE

France in a recreation of the early flights at the beginning of the last century. It seemed all very tedious to me, and I was even more bored when one of the assistant directors announced that we were going to do it all over again that afternoon by re-dressing the airfield so they could pretend it was in France, where the aircraft in the film 'arrived'.

I was pretty fed up by this stage because I wasn't even earning any money. I'd gone along with my mum and aunts literally for the ride because the chance of a two-hour trip in the Zodiac was far too good to miss.

I was hanging around the catering van when I was suddenly hauled out of the crowd by an assistant and told I was going to be a 'featured artist' in the film. I didn't really know what he was talking about. Then he told me my face would be seen on camera and I'd be paid *seven guineas*, as opposed to the two guineas my mother and aunts were getting for being extras.

My mother looked very irritated as I disappeared off to the wardrobe tent, where I was decked out in a tweed jacket and a yellow corduroy deerstalker, which made me look like Sherlock Holmes' plump illegitimate lovechild.

A few minutes later I was positioned standing on the running board of a 1923 Bentley 3-Litre Sport in that oversized tweed jacket and deerstalker, and if you don't blink you can spot me halfway through the movie. The 1923 Bentley 3-Litre Sport was a noisy old devil and I didn't really appreciate its classic lines. It was all quite boring, as they insisted on doing ten takes of my scene, but I did enjoy the way my mother got in a right strop because I got paid so much more than her. She never took me on another film shoot after that. I wonder why. But my abiding memory was of that magnificent car. The film business was a bore, but at least I'd been paid enough to buy a dozen of my favourite bang-up-to-date Corgi model cars.

PASSENGER GEORGE TO THE RESCUE

THROUGHOUT MY CHILDHOOD I OFTEN RETREATED INTO MY motoring netherworld to avoid the domestic chaos going on at home. But despite all my parents' rows and sulks, my mother and father continued to give out a vibe that seemed to say: 'It's us against the world.'

I remember one time my father disappeared off to Italy for a few weeks on some sort of work assignment, or so he told us. But looking back on it now, I suspect he was either taking a break from home or he had a girlfriend tucked away somewhere.

My mother looked crestfallen when he announced he was off to Italy over breakfast one morning. I could sense the tension in the air, and my mother's complete lack of response to his announcement spoke volumes for how she felt.

My dad departed a few minutes later with an awkward wave and headed off to the airport in a car driven by his company chauffeur, Eric. The atmosphere in the house immediately darkened, and my mother retired to bed almost immediately after breakfast.

I retreated up to my bedroom and pulled out all my favourite Corgi and Dinky cars and started trying to recreate the Monte Carlo Rally on my carpet. I knew it was going to be difficult while my dad was away, and I worried about my mother because I knew she'd start drinking even more heavily and neglecting herself if he wasn't coming home from work every night.

I didn't clap eyes on her for the next two days. I'd creep past her bedroom on the middle floor of the house and go down to the ground-floor kitchen to grill myself some sausages, or maybe heat up a tin of beans, or make my special treat to myself of cheese on toast. Throughout, the Zodiac just sat there outside the house, virtually taunting me.

Every now and again the phone would ring, and I could hear her wearily picking it up and saying a few flat and toneless words before the receiver was clicked back into place. I had no doubt a bottle of gin and a lot of Tuinal tranquillisers were being consumed behind the closed doors of her bedroom.

Two mornings after my father's departure, I was having breakfast on my own at the huge dining-room table when the doorbell went. It was a delivery man with a smallish cardboard box. He didn't seem bothered by the fact I was just a kid and kindly accepted my signature in exchange for the package, even though it was addressed to my mother. It was odd because there was no label on it so I had no idea what it contained, but it was quite light and it had a very strange synthetic smell to it.

But my mother had long since taught me not to pry into other people's lives because you'd be sure to find something you didn't want to find. She'd never snoop through a diary of mine or open one of my letters so I wasn't about to do the same to her, even though I was very curious about that cardboard box.

I shook it carefully a couple of times, but there were no immediate clues except that it was quite light, so I carried it up to her bedroom door and knocked gently before going in.

It was 9.30 in the morning and she was fast asleep in a pink dressing gown, with her head slumped to one side on the pillow and a half-empty bottle of gin on the bedside table next to her. Her eyes fluttered open and she looked straight at me. I could tell from her expression that she wished I wasn't seeing her in this state.

PASSENGER GEORGE TO THE RESCUE

I placed the cardboard box on the end of the bed and left the room without uttering a word. I knew she was upset about my father going away, and when she went into one of these moods it was always better just to retreat and leave her in her own little world, from which she would eventually emerge.

I spent most of the rest of the day designing and then drawing new car models on my own on that same vast dining-room table. The atmosphere in the house felt as flat as a pancake, and the silence was only occasionally broken by the noise of a tenant quietly moving through the hallway on their way in or out of the house.

My mother was bedridden and knocking herself unconscious twice a day with sedatives and alcohol. I, meanwhile, was bored out of my head and in desperate need of some visual stimulation. Our big cumbersome black-and-white telly in the sitting room had conked out the previous afternoon, and I didn't even have enough money to slip out to the corner shop and buy myself the latest Corgi.

That night I put myself to bed after sharing a hot chocolate and some ginger nuts with elderly tenant Miss Hogg as she banged on and on about the good old days before the First World War. I didn't sleep well that night because I was worried about my mother and I had a feeling she was going to do something even crazier than usual.

The following morning I was awoken as ever by the onslaught of the early-morning rush hour as cars thundered past our front door on their way into central London. I was always super-sensitive to the sound of certain cars, so I'd often just lie there and visualise many of the cars driving past, recognising specific models from the tone of their engines. And I had my clear favourites. The deep, rumbling sound of the V6 of a Triumph TR3 came top of that list. I never quite worked out why that V6 on the Triumph sounded different from so many other virtually identical engines. Maybe it was the size of the vehicle itself because it was a relatively small car for such a big engine. Another big favourite was the Austin-Healey, which had a cool, soft yet powerful tone. But of course these engines were easy to fit to a name because they weren't your common-or-garden everyday saloons. Mind you, I could tell an MG 1100 from a Mini Cooper any day, even though to most people they must have sounded virtually identical.

CAR TROUBLE

So there I was lying in bed, listening avidly to the sound of all these cars tearing down my road. Luckily it kept me diverted for a while, because I was dreading another boring day at home with a mother who was in danger of becoming west London's answer to Howard Hughes.

Suddenly I heard the unmistakable sound of my mother's Zodiac firing up outside. I sat bolt upright in bed for a second to continue listening in case I'd got it wrong, but there was no mistaking that sound. I jumped out of bed and headed straight to the window, where a dozen lazy, fat pigeons were waiting for their daily bread. I yanked open the sash window and shooed them away so I could get a closer look.

It crossed my mind that someone might be stealing our car. Our pride and joy. The one thing I was more proud of than anything else. I'd read in the *Daily Mirror* that Zodiacs were popular with bank robbers and other criminal types and that they were second only to another Ford, the Cortina, as the most stolen car in Britain.

All this stuff was rushing through my panicked little head as I strained to look down to see what was happening with the Zodiac. I could just make out the exhaust fumes coming from the back as the car ticked over. Surely a car thief would just put their foot down and get the hell out of there as fast as possible?

When the Zodiac moved off with a bit of jerk, I knew immediately that my mother must have been at the wheel. She always set off in exactly the same way, stopping very briefly to check for oncoming traffic then smashing her foot down so as to beat anything careering round the corner from the other end of our street.

That's when I saw him: the unmistakable shape of a man sitting next to her. I got a full sideways view as the Zodiac powered off to the right and up the road. I was completely thrown. I never heard anybody come in the house during the night, apart from the tenants, and I knew – just like I knew the sound of the cars – the sound of their individual footsteps. No one else had been in or out of the house. I was convinced of that.

Not only had she gone on a drive without me – and believe me, I would have given anything just to get out of the house at that stage

– but she had a man who was not my father with her. A wave of insecurity came over me. It was a confusing feeling for a child, but I knew something was badly wrong. I wished my father would hurry up and come home.

I must have walked up and down the kitchen about a thousand times that morning, waiting for my mother to return to the house. Every few minutes I'd check out of the bay window to see if there was any sign of the Zodiac.

I didn't dare leave the house in case she returned, and I kept worrying about who that mystery man was and why he was with my mother. To say it was driving me to distraction would have been a complete understatement. The tenants came and went, but by lunchtime there was still no sign of her.

Then the phone went, and it was my father in Italy. He sounded quite nervy, and I was lost for words when he asked me how everything was at home. I missed him desperately because I didn't like what was happening at home in his absence, but I knew not to say anything. Like any child caught up in a domestic dispute, I didn't want to cause any more problems between my parents. Then my father asked if my mother was there, and I didn't know how to respond. For a few moments I said nothing.

'Hello. Are you still there?' he asked.

I said I had to go because someone was at the front door, and I'd get my mother to call him. But he said not to bother because he was 'moving around' – whatever that meant – and he'd ring the next day.

I put the phone down and turned to look once again through the window, and there she was, reversing the Zodiac into our carport. *And that man was still sitting next to her*. I gulped and waited for a moment before deciding what to do. Then I dashed towards the front door. I felt a mixture of indignation and relief. I didn't like the way I felt about that man and what he was doing with my mother, but my overwhelming concern was her well-being, and at least she was back in one piece.

As I ran two at a time down the front steps, she slowly emerged, a little the worse for wear, but nowhere near as wobbly as I'd seen her so many times in the past. She smiled faintly in my direction but didn't even look behind her as I waited for her 'friend' to emerge.

But he didn't seem to be budging. Why wasn't he getting out of the Zodiac? It didn't make sense. I leaned further down and looked through the rear passenger window to see what he was doing. He wasn't moving. I glanced at my mother quizzically, but that inane smile remained and it always told me not to ask awkward questions.

So I looked back through the passenger window at her 'friend'. He didn't look back at me. In fact, he didn't even acknowledge me in any shape or form. He wasn't moving an inch.

The smile on my mother's face broadened into one of her classic Cheshire Cat specials, and she leaned back into the car and dragged the 'man' out through her open doorway. 'He' was a blow-up doll, and his 'body' only went down to the waist.

'Meet George,' said my mum. That was it. No other introduction. No explanation of why 'George' even existed.

God knows why she'd decided to drive round London with a blow-up man next to her, but I was so relieved that I put all such questions to the back of my mind and simply laughed nervously along with her. She then pulled the tiny rubber plug out of him, and we giggled while listening to the farting sound of the air escaping.

By the time we got to the kitchen, 'George' was no more than a crumpled-up mass of grey- and flesh-coloured plastic. It was only then it finally dawned on me that 'he' must have been in the box that had been delivered to the house a couple of days earlier. But I still didn't have a clue why she'd got him in the first place.

A couple of hours later I sauntered down to the kitchen for something to eat, and there was my mum and one of her sisters having a right laugh at someone's expense. Then I noticed that 'George' had been reinflated and he was sitting at the head of the dining-room table while my mum and aunt were puffing away on cigarettes and supping whisky in tumblers.

My aunt Mary winked at me as I opened the fridge door, and I smiled back because it was always reassuring to see her in the house, especially when my mother was on her own.

Just then the phone went in the sitting room. I rushed to answer it in the hope it would be my father because I felt much more at ease about talking to him now I knew my mother was okay and there was no other man on the scene.

But my father barely acknowledged me and asked to 'speak to your mother immediately'. It was rare that he ever sounded annoyed so I was puzzled and a bit thrown by his attitude.

My mother appeared in the sitting room looking as serene as ever. True, she'd had a couple of drinks to calm her nerves. And I could tell she was on the edge of one of those feisty, wind-up moods where she could turn on anyone at any time, apart from her sister, who she always adored.

'Hello,' she mumbled slightly drunkenly into the phone. There was a beat of silence, then I heard my father's voice. He boomed at her: 'Where the bloody hell have you been?' And that was only the beginning.

I retreated back into the kitchen, where my aunt raised her eyebrows and slowly shut the door to block out the shouting. It became muffled and hard to distinguish, but I knew that my mother and father were having one of their periodic humdingers. I pretended to need to go to the loo so my aunt would let me out of the kitchen.

I shot up the stairs to the first landing and then sat on the top step and listened avidly. It turned out my mother had bought 'George' to wind my father up because he had gone off to Italy and she suspected he was with another woman. So the previous evening she'd put him in my father's seat at the head of the dining table, left the front bay-window curtains open and then called my father's company chauffeur, Eric, to come over to pick her up for a party, except there was no party. She just wanted the chauffeur to see 'George' in the window and presume she was entertaining a 'gentleman friend'. So after sending Eric the chauffeur away, she packed George in his box until the following morning, when she blew him up again and plonked him in the passenger seat of the Zodiac. Then she took George on a tour of the area near my father's office in Stamford Street, Waterloo, and made sure that as many of his work colleagues as possible spotted her cruising around with 'another man' in the seat next to her in the

CAR TROUBLE

Zodiac that many at my father's newspaper, *Reveille*, knew so well.

Well, it certainly had the desired effect because my father soon heard from his workmates that my mother was out in the Zodiac with a 'young man'.

I stayed up at the top of that first flight of stairs until after my mother had finished talking to my father. As she breezed through the hall on the way back to the kitchen, she looked up at me and laughed. It was a manic, slightly drunken laugh, but she didn't care because the most important thing was that she'd taught my father a lesson he would never forget.

I rushed down the stairs after she went into the kitchen just in time to hear my mother telling my aunt Mary: 'He's getting the first plane back tomorrow morning.'

Then she clinked whisky tumblers with my aunt and they both downed a triple in one gulp.

PILE-UP

BESIDES BEING A NUT FOR CARS THAT BELONGED TO THE current day, I was also fascinated by the history of the motor car and the fact that when my dad was born in 1912 there were hardly any on the road, especially in his homeland of New Zealand. I didn't actually ask him much about it, but it preyed on my mind because I couldn't imagine a world without cars. It must have been so weird.

My closest link to the history of motor cars actually came through the old lady tenant called Miss Hogg. Years later I found she was a former brothel keeper who'd become a star witness for the police after quitting 'the game' just after the end of the Second World War. She was at least 80 in the early 1960s, so I guess that means she was born in about 1880.

I'd spend hours in her room – on the same floor as my bedroom – listening to her talking about the good old days when the maximum speed of cars was about 20 mph. That seemed painfully slow to me because speed was the key ingredient for a kid obsessed with cars. Cars used to race down our one-way street at about 50 or even 60 mph. There were no restrictions and lots of deaths as a result. I know because I got myself a stopwatch and used to calculate their speeds sometimes over a specific distance.

CAR TROUBLE

I remember one time I was happily ensconced in Miss Hogg's bedsit when there was an almighty bang from out front that got me jumping up and rushing to my bedroom window, which overlooked our road. Three cars had smashed into each other and there was steam and smoke and people seemed to be hanging out of the windscreens of two of the cars.

I rushed down the four flights of stairs to the ground floor and dashed straight out into the street to see if I could help. It was a dreadful scene of carnage and destruction.

I stood there on the pavement, not really knowing what to do because other pedestrians were trying to pull the people out of the cars. Miss Hogg finally appeared alongside me and looked completely uninterested by what had happened. 'If they'd stuck to a sensible speed, this would never have happened,' she said. I was so engrossed in watching two pedestrians trying to pull a man out of the side window of his car that I didn't really absorb what she was saying.

But like any enthusiast, I wasn't put off driving by the carnage I witnessed that afternoon. On the contrary, it just made me feel even more determined to drive because it seemed so exciting.

WEIRD CAR THAT WOULDN'T SINK

CLEARLY SCHOOL HAD LITTLE APPEAL TO ME FROM AN EARLY age. I much preferred it at home, either in my little room at the top of the house, hemmed in by that strange collection of sitting tenants, or out in the Zodiac, pretending to drive. I hated meeting the tenants on the stairs or coming out of the bathroom on the landing, but at least if any baddies came through the window or broke in downstairs when my parents were out on the town, then they'd protect me. Well, I certainly hoped they would.

I always got myself up every morning for school. I never had any problems getting out of bed, but then all the tenants that surrounded me were usually up early for work, which meant the queue at the bathroom could be as many as three people, and they all used to wait there to make sure they didn't lose their place. I used to spend ages gazing out of the hall window next to the bathroom down at the refuse yard behind our house, watching all the dustbin lorries charging in and out, dumping all the stinking rubbish in a huge pile that backed onto the wall at the end of our garden. I got to recognise the dustmen from watching them working away in the yard and then spotting the same characters on the lorries when they appeared in our street emptying dustbins.

Sometimes I felt like saying hello to some of these characters because it was as if I knew them from watching them in the yard. But, of course, they had no idea who I was so it would have seemed pretty weird if I had. I even gave some of them nicknames because of the way they looked. One morning I actually spotted two of them having a fight in the yard when I was waiting patiently for my turn in the bathroom. It was a vicious fight, but later that same day both men were out in the dustbin lorry with black eyes, and it felt weird knowing what had happened. It was almost as if I knew the secrets of their lives, even though they didn't know who I was.

From the age of about seven I managed to get away with regularly bunking off school, often by forging a letter, which I'd post to the headmaster. I got away with it by adapting a couple of original earlier letters from my mother, which I'd made a point of replicating specifically for this purpose. I seemed to almost have a criminal's mindset about such things from a disturbingly young age. There was always so much stuff going on in my head, though.

As I've mentioned before, the highlight of my early education was reading the *Daily Mirror* every morning and playing Capital Cities with my father on the way to school. At least I was already highly educated when it came to cars. My dad thought my obsession with them was just a passing phase, but he knew I was very knowledgeable about them and one day he asked me if I had any ideas for a competition for the readers of his newspaper.

A good competition would be one where I won loads of cars and kept them all to myself. But back in the real world, I liked the challenge of coming up with an idea for my father so I put a lot of time and effort into thinking about it.

Knowing my dad's fears about driving, caused by him being in those amphibious landing craft at Dunkirk, then gave me a brilliant idea. The German-made Amphicar had just been launched, which was a modern-day amphibious car with long, straight tail fins and two propellers sticking out under the boot. The tabloids were fascinated by it. I longed for a ride in one, just to see if it really worked or whether it was all a big con and would sink like a stone the moment it drove into the water. I suggested to my dad that his newspaper hold a competition to give one away. My dad was so delighted with my idea as we walked to school that morning that he promised to get me a proper ride in one after his marketing people had lined up a free one for the competition, which featured a question for *Reveille* readers along the lines of: 'What is the capital of the United States of America: New York, Washington or Los Angeles?' I was really chuffed to have come up with an idea my dad liked.

But my happiness didn't last long. That feeling of dread about school was never far away. It really seemed a brutal, trying place, and I'd always felt the odd one out there.

As I climbed the steep steps up to the school's front door a few mornings later, I wished as usual that I was bunking off. It all felt like such a waste of time. I wandered into the hallway, secretly praying that one of the nicer teachers (there were only two) would suddenly come up to me and announce school was postponed for the day.

At that moment, I got a familiar tap on my shoulder. I slowly turned to face the headmaster's son, who was my chief tormenter at school. He was about 30 and sometimes even walked around the classrooms clutching a cane, in his capacity as 'deputy head'.

I took a big gulp of air and tried to smile up at him, which was hard for all sorts of reasons, including the fact he was well over six feet tall and towered over all of us.

'I've got something for you, Clarkson,' he said in a very menacing tone.

I didn't know what to reply at first so I just nodded.

I presumed I was in trouble with a capital 'T'. But then I was used to my fair share of punishments and detentions so nothing would surprise me.

Then he pushed a letter into my hand. I was panic-stricken. What was it? What had I done now? Hey. Maybe they wanted me to leave the school. What a relief that would be.

'Strange that you should get a letter addressed here instead of your home,' he said, suspiciously.

It wasn't a normal-looking letter, either. It had a see-through window with my name and the address of the school typed out neatly. It was all very confusing. I looked over hesitantly at the headmaster's son. He was peering down at me, willing me to open the letter in his presence.

'Aren't you going to open it, then?'

Something was stopping me from doing it, even though I knew it was infuriating him. Why should I share the contents of that letter with someone I loathed? So I walked away without even acknowledging his last comment. I could feel his irritated gaze right on me, but I left him fuming.

A few minutes later I found a quiet corner in the school refectory and pulled the mystery letter out again and began opening it carefully. I didn't want to end up damaging whatever was actually inside the envelope.

It turned out to be a cheque for three guineas made out to my name and signed by the editor of *Reveille*, my father. The invoice said: 'Boat Car competition idea'.

He'd paid me like an adult for my idea, and it was the best letter I'd ever opened in my life. I really felt ten feet tall after I read it. I had finally achieved something, which really surprised me and made me realise for the first time in my life how nice it was to be appreciated.

MY FRIEND PUFFY AND A ZEPHYR

MY HIDING PLACE IN THE FAMILY CAR IN FRONT OF THE HOUSE
had long since been discovered so I sometimes headed off in the
direction of the local parks to avoid my horrible school when I left
home of a morning. On the way I'd walk via the small Bristol car
showroom round the corner and gaze for ages at the vehicles. They
featured a 405 just like the one that had almost run me over on my
way to school when I was a bit younger.

I liked the Bristols because they were shaped like chunky bullets,
with massive smiling grilles, and Paul Jones, the lead singer from my
favourite group, Manfred Mann, drove one, according to the *Daily
Mirror*. I adored their 1964 hit single 'Do Wah Diddy Diddy'.

Bristols were promoted as being 'handcrafted' so I convinced myself
that one little man spent years making each car in a little lock-up
somewhere. The Bristols had these huge, thick chrome bumpers, which
were always being polished by young apprentices in pristine white
overalls whenever I passed the showroom. I'd often stand there with
my school uniform hidden under a huge anorak, and my brown-leather
satchel strapped round my back, just staring at them. I remember one
time the huge sliding glass doors to the showroom opened and a 405

glided out onto the street. It was really strange seeing one of them actually moving after studying them in the showroom for so long. I'd started to convince myself they were fake showroom models that didn't actually have engines.

Usually I'd then head off to one of the nearby parks for a wander. *Anything* was better than going to school. I didn't like talking to strangers because I was far too shy and suspicious of people's motives to let them engage me. I'd often smuggle some bread crusts out of the kitchen at home and fling them at the ducks on the pond at Kensington Gardens.

Then I'd find a nice sheltered bench, pull my favourite toy – the Etch A Sketch – out of my satchel and start designing brand-new cars, occasionally looking up as the traffic moved sluggishly along the main road through the middle of the park. I'd focus on particular parts of the passing vehicles. I'd spot a Rover 3.5-Litre and quickly sketch out its rear wing and back light, and then I'd see a Humber and do the same with its front grille and so on, until I had created my own brand-new model of car, which would feature all those elements from the cars that I was watching from the park.

The biggest problem with the Etch A Sketch was that each time I did a drawing it would disappear if I moved at all because that was the point of the toy. You shook it and started again. In the end I got frustrated by it and started taking along an exercise book as well and drawing new car models by pencil from the Etch A Sketch before I wiped the pictures off the machine.

I do sometimes wonder why I liked that toy so much when all it did was wipe away my memories and achievements, but maybe that's the exact reason why: because whenever I shook that toy, *everything* disappeared. It was how I often wished my life would evolve, in a sense.

Eventually I'd get bored of park life and head onto Kensington High Street to do some shopping. Well, what I really mean is shoplifting. My pocket money barely stretched to one toy car back then so it was only natural to do a bit of shoplifting for Corgi and Dinky cars, as well as the occasional Airfix model aeroplane, which I could never be bothered to finish.

MY FRIEND PUFFY AND A ZEPHYR

I usually targeted the huge toy department at Barkers, on Kensington High Street, as opposed to the smaller store at the end of my street, for obvious reasons. The first time I went 'lifting' was probably the only time when I nearly got caught.

I was in Barkers stupidly circling round and round the toy-car section, trying to build up the courage to swipe a two-tone Zephyr estate police car that caught my eye. I should have looked highly suspicious to anyone passing, but luckily the sight of a rather scruffy eight-year-old in a baggy blue raincoat over flannel shorts didn't attract much attention. Then I convinced myself I'd been spotted by one particularly beady-looking shop assistant. But in fact it turned out he was looking next to me at a rather pretty girl. When I finally worked this out, I darted my hand out like a lizard's tongue, grabbed the Corgi box and pushed it into my satchel. It was all over in a split second. I looked around in a very uncool manner and then pulled the peak down on my school hat as if that would somehow help me avoid being spotted.

I then started walking very fast towards the lift inside the huge store before I suddenly realised I had to slow down. It must have been so obvious, but there were no hands on my shoulders telling me that my game was up, so I continued.

I pressed on the lift button frantically, but tried not to look up in case any of the other shoppers nearby noticed the glazed look of panic in my eyes. The elevator seemed to take hours to arrive, and I was soon sweating and shaking. I kept pressing on the plastic button over and over, like some spoilt, impatient little brat.

When the doors finally opened, I was faced with a completely full lift. I couldn't believe it. I turned and looked back at the toy department, and no one seemed to have even noticed anything had been stolen. After the lift doors closed, I thought maybe I should put the toy car back and then no one would be any the wiser. I'd been thinking that for approximately two seconds when another elevator arrived and I decided to push on.

The sweat was bucketing off me, but I finally got downstairs to the hallway of Barkers. As I darted towards the huge double exit doors, a commissionaire type in a peaked hat with a white rim seemed to be looking me up and down. After all this effort I was going to get nabbed by some old boy with a handlebar moustache and a couple of meaningless epaulettes. I kept walking, but I knew he was watching me very closely so I just kept moving and did not look back.

A few seconds later, I stopped on a corner of Kensington High Street and felt inside my satchel to see if the Zephyr estate was still there. I was actually starting to wonder if I'd imagined the whole shoplifting scene. Then, as the realisation dawned, I felt an extraordinary surge of adrenalin rushing through me. I'd just got away with something quite momentous and the feeling was out of this world. I'd want to replicate that excitement more and more and more in the future.

I floated home that afternoon and announced to my mother I was home early from school because one of the teachers was sick. It was a pathetic excuse, but she made no attempt to question it, let alone call up the school to find out what would have happened if they'd sent me home to an empty house.

I was pleased as punch with my Ford Zephyr police car, especially since my mother was always claiming that 'they'd never make a shooting brake version' (that's what they often called them back in those days) because of course we had the Zodiac saloon, which was almost identical. I was looking forward to the next day, when I'd pull it out of my pocket and tell her she was wrong.

But that afternoon I went straight up to my room, took the Zephyr shooting brake out of my satchel and held it up in the window while looking down at my mother's real, life-size Zodiac saloon parked outside. The toy version looked as if someone at Corgi had just welded half a tiny metal box onto the back of the standard Zephyr saloon. Oh well.

I put the toy car down on the ledge and opened the window just wide enough for me to spread some old bits of bread out for the pigeons. Seconds later, five or six – including a huge fat one I'd nicknamed Puffy – came fluttering down for their food. Moments later, a pack of cars came racing round the corner towards our house, making so much noise that the pigeons got scared and flew away. It was one of the few times in my life when I wished that cars did not exist.

A 'CAT' IN BRITISH RACING GREEN . . .

ONE WINTER'S MORNING, MY FATHER UNCHARACTERISTICALLY insisted on walking with me to the toyshop on the corner of our street. My money was burning a hole in my pocket because I wanted to get a Corgi version of James Bond's gold Aston Martin DB5, complete with its own ejector passenger seat and rear bulletproof screen. I'd sneaked into the local Odeon to see *Thunderball* a few days earlier.

That day there was an awkward silence between us and I knew something was up, but it was only as we got closer to the toyshop that my father blurted it out: 'Your mother's going to India for six months to see her father, but I'll be staying here.'

I didn't respond and just upped the pace to try to get to the toyshop even faster. My dad felt so bad about it all that he insisted on paying for 007's Aston Martin. That meant I could also afford to buy a toy *Stingray*, like the one from the TV programme, which you could wind up so it cruised below the surface of the bathwater. It was only when I got home and flopped on my bed that what my father had said actually sunk in, and I began crying into my pillow. Luckily neither of my parents heard me.

CAR TROUBLE

Those six months when my mother was away went very slowly, and I spent a lot of my time sitting in the front seat of the Zodiac, which she'd left unlocked, trying my hardest to drive it in the direction of India. I searched high and low for the car keys, but luckily never found them. I got the occasional postcard from my mother, which mentioned little more than the weather. Meanwhile my aunts – her two unmarried sisters – cooked me huge suppers and encouraged me to stay with them, even though their flat was just round the corner from our house. They were always careful never to mention my brother, whom I found out many years later had died in his cot.

Both aunts ran stalls in two London antiques markets, and I sometimes worked as their assistant, even bunking off school to go with them to Bermondsey Market, in south-east London, at the crack of dawn on Friday mornings. My aunt's bright-red three-door VW Variant shooting brake intrigued me because it was an estate car with only three doors, instead of the usual five. The VW Variant 'squareback', as it was known, was supposed to be ahead of its time with its modern, water-cooled design, but the front engine sounded like my Action Man gargling with nails. And the only person who could possibly look cool in this two-door shooting brake was Noddy.

I was already putting all these childhood memories into a box that could only be unlocked if they had a link to my obsession with cars.

One day, six months later, my mother simply appeared at the front door while my father and I were having breakfast. I ran to greet her in the hallway, and she gave me a peck on the cheek before sitting down at the breakfast table and pouring herself a cup of coffee, as if she'd just returned from buying some cigarettes at the corner shop.

I was very excited, mainly because it meant we could go out for drives in the Zodiac once again. My father said virtually nothing, although I remember noticing he was beaming from ear to ear. My mother just carried on sipping her cup of coffee, but hardly said a word. Looking back on it, it all seemed quite surreal. She seemed to me to be in some sort of strange 'soft focus' all the time. It was as if she was there, but she wasn't *all* there, if that makes any sense. And

I never even asked how the grandfather I had never met was because I knew that was irrelevant.

My mother gave off this flatness, which stopped me ever asking her any questions about what really happened in India. I just happily accepted her return and we got on with our respective lives. I was definitely really glad she was back, so I guess that must have meant I missed her, although I didn't want to admit any of that to her at the time.

My dad duly celebrated my mother's return by wangling a new company car from Daily Mirror Newspapers, even though my mother was the only driver in the family. It turned out to be a brand-new British racing green automatic Jaguar 3.4 Mark II with a top speed of 138 mph. I vividly remember that 'cat' purring softly when my mother fired up the V6 engine for the first time after a huge car transporter turned up one afternoon and unloaded it outside our house. Equally importantly, the Jag just happened to be in my *top three* of those vehicles I logged when they passed our house. It was so exciting to know that my mother now had one of these beautifully sleek motorised beasts.

India and all that heartbreak were soon forgotten in a haze of car excitement.

THIS IS THE SECOND PART!

On the deck of the biggest vessel I ever steered.

THE DAY A JAG REALLY PURRED . . .

MY MOTHER MADE A REAL EFFORT TO BE NICE TO ME AFTER she got back from India. Within days of taking delivery of the new Jag, we went out together for a drive through the countryside. I'd dusted down my toy steering wheel and attached it to the back of her seat, and we were both screeching round some hairy country lanes. Before she'd gone to India, I'd loved leaning across as the car swerved round corners, but now the toy steering wheel seemed a bit childish to me. During those six months that my mother had been away, I'd grown even more obsessed with actually driving a *real* car, thanks to all those sessions sitting in the Zodiac while it was parked in front of our home. That day I caught my mother's eye at a set of traffic lights. 'Hey. I thought you were driving,' she said, looking straight at me in the mirror.

I didn't answer, but just gave out a huge sigh and grumpily folded my arms together. She knew what I really wanted to do.

A few minutes later, my mother flicked off the Beatles track on the radio and turned the Jag into the open entrance of a muddy field and came to a halt. I was bemused and very worried about the Jag getting dirty. Without saying a word, she leaned over the back of her seat and handed me a pillow. Then she got out of the driver's seat and climbed in the back. I completely froze for a few moments while looking at that pillow in my lap, and then I took a deep breath and clambered over into the driver's seat.

After I'd carefully adjusted the seat and that pillow, my mother calmly leaned between the two front seats and pulled the column change down to 'D' for Drive. The car immediately began creeping forward. I was confused at first because I'd thought I'd have to accelerate to make it move.

'Now slowly press your right foot on the right-hand pedal,' said my mother, in a remarkably calm voice, considering a nine-year-old child was at the wheel of a car. No doubt a few Tuinal tranquillisers were helping cool her nerves.

I gingerly looked down to check on the pedal. Then I pushed my foot on it, almost standing up in the process, and the Jag roared up; the bonnet virtually seemed to lift off the ground. In the back seat, my mother was swigging on a Dettol bottle, which was secretly filled with whisky. I was petrified by the way the Jag responded so I immediately took my foot off the pedal and the engine idled, although the car continued to creep forward very slowly.

'Put your foot on it more gently,' she slurred between puffs on a cigarette and further swigs of Dettol. She might just as well have been teaching me a salsa dance step.

This time I got the message and stroked the pedal much more softly with my foot. I held on very tightly to the wobbling steering wheel as the Jag bobbed along on the muddy field, occasionally squelching through cowpats and molehills. Despite the pillow and being tall for my age, I could only just see through the misty windscreen. My eyes were fixed on the Jaguar 'leaper' on the bonnet, which had become almost like a rifle sight with which to point myself in the right direction. I had no clue where we were actually going, although my mother didn't seem to care, which just about summed up our life together.

Suddenly the Jag veered alarmingly to the right as we drove over a ridge in the field. I should have braked, but I wasn't confident enough to do it so I continued driving, and somehow we 'rode' over that ridge despite a huge bump and a clunk from the undercarriage.

THE DAY A JAG REALLY PURRED...

As we carried on – half sliding and half driving at a strange angle – I started to feel more confident and pressed slightly harder on the accelerator pedal. The Jag hit 10 mph, which was quite fast on a bumpy, sloping field. I remember the speed very well because my eyes kept darting between the speedometer and the rifle-sight 'leaper' on the bonnet. Ever since a young age I had always checked parked-car speedometers in the street to see what the last number was on the dial. There was a 160 mph limit mark on the Jag 3.4 Mark II. *One hundred and sixty miles per hour.* It was scary just thinking about that speed.

My eyes were so fixated on the speedometer at that moment that I didn't notice a couple of sheep wandering slowly towards us. Then I suddenly spotted them out of the corner of my eye. It was a terrifying reality check. I had to consider the safety of others for the first time while driving. I stamped my foot hard on the enormous brake pedal and was immediately thrown hard against the steering wheel, sending the Jag slewing to a halt in the mud at a precarious angle.

Moments later the sheep sleepily wandered by without even giving us a second glance as my mother coolly leaned in between the two green-leather front bucket seats and nonchalantly flicked the column change to 'P' for Park. Then she got out of the back, opened the driver's door and, smiling down at me with those gappy front teeth, gave me a big hug, which was really nice and rather unusual for her. But most important of all, she'd just given me an unshakable confidence in my own driving ability. Nothing would stop me now.

STEERING THE BIGGEST 'CAR' EVER

THAT SUMMER OF 1966 ENGLAND WON THE WORLD CUP, AND I watched it on my own at home while my parents were out at some party or other.

As usual, my mother continued to look for escape routes to alleviate her boredom. She hated being alone when my father was working long hours so she was always creating her own special adventures. I think in many ways, encouraging me how to drive at such an early age was part of that adventurous spirit. She loved defying the world, whether it was refusing to use car indicators or smoking men's cigars. It was the same with holidays and travelling. We first went to Spain when hardly anyone from Britain had even dreamt of going there. But when Spain became too popular, my mother decided on some much more bizarre destinations.

So it was that one Saturday morning when I was nine or ten, I ventured downstairs for what I expected to be my usual lonely breakfast and was pleasantly surprised to find her poring over a map spread across the dining-room table. I thought at first she was planning one of her classic road-trips, but then when I looked a bit closer I noticed it was a map of the whole of northern Europe, Scandinavia and the western Soviet Union. Surely she wasn't planning to drive across all those countries?

As usual, my mother didn't offer much explanation. I wandered over to the cooker and put some toast under the grill. 'We're going on a trip,' she finally volunteered in a slightly jumpy, jolly voice that sounded like she'd already popped a few happy pills. I was concentrating on spreading a wodge of butter on my toast at that moment and waiting for the milk to boil for my hot chocolate, so it was my turn not to react immediately. It wasn't until about a minute later that her words finally sank in.

'A trip? Where?'

She didn't answer so I just nodded my head and said nothing else in case she brought me crashing down to earth with a disappointing reply. Less was more when it came to my mother, and this was one of those typical moments. I was imagining an exciting flight in an aeroplane. I really loved flying. That could have meant anywhere from Calais to Moscow, but I didn't care as long as it got us out of the house. I was also delighted because if we were about to go on 'a trip' it fell right in the middle of the winter term, and I hated school, as my mother knew only too well.

Anyway, my mother sloped off upstairs to her bedroom clutching a super-strong two-spoonful cup of Nescafé, while I sat there imagining myself boarding a VC10, *the* trendiest aircraft for long-distance travel from Heathrow in those days. I'd already been on a Trident to Spain on one holiday and they were a bit like mini-VC10s so I presumed the VC10 with its engines at the back would be similar to fly in. I rather liked the way the Trident surged into the air at a steep angle because of the position of those engines.

Once again I was being recruited as my mother's sidekick. If no one else was around, I'd do, and, quite frankly, I played along because I wanted to escape as much as she did.

My mother didn't utter another word about our 'trip' that day. But I packed my own suitcase just in case she suddenly announced we were off at the crack of dawn the following morning. I dug out a rather nice little black-canvas British European Airways holdall bag to use as hand luggage.

I still hadn't a clue why or precisely where we were going, so I just delved into my imagination and planned out the whole trip in my head. But I did start fretting that my BEA holdall might get me arrested if we strayed beyond European borders. Maybe the customs guards would confiscate the bag? That night I tried to shut my eyes and get some sleep, but I was way too excited, so I went into 'car mode' and counted the cars passing the house in the same way some people count sheep in their heads. Eventually I nodded off as the traffic outside turned into nothing more than a dribble.

Next morning I was woken as early as ever by the noise of the traffic once again building up for the rush hour. It was strangely reassuring to be woken by the sound of engines. It always helped me recover quickly from a nasty, vivid nightmare because the noise reminded me that I was back in the land of the living.

The first thing I'd do most mornings was crumble a bit of old bread that sat in a bag by the window and then spread it out onto the ledge for my friends the pigeons to devour. Then I'd pick up my exercise book and check the most popular models of cars that I'd noted down the previous day racing past the house.

But on that morning after my mother's vague announcement about a 'trip', I had other things on my mind. I wanted to get to discover exactly where we were actually going. No child likes uncertainty, and in that sense I was no different from the rest.

I'd just got to the bottom of the stairs when I spotted a large envelope on the hall table with a buff-coloured letter poking out from one end, as if my mother had opened it and then left it there in a hurry. Now, as I've said previously, I didn't pry into my parents' business, but on this occasion I was on a 'mission' so I couldn't resist a peek. Looking back on it, I think maybe my mother left that opened envelope out deliberately for me to discover so she didn't have to go through the tedious process of explaining stuff to me.

I knew they were tickets when I got close to the hall table because our passports were also there. The tickets actually turned out to be buff-coloured card with bright-green writing, which was unusual. I turned them round the right way up and noticed the name on the top: 'Balticline'. I guessed it must have been the name of some foreign airline and it sounded Scandinavian, so now I had an idea where we were going. Then I looked closer and stopped for a moment. There was no mention of an airport and we were flying from somewhere called Tilbury, which – thanks to my father's geography lessons on the way to school – I knew was a port on the Thames. Hang on, we're going on a 'trip' *by ship*.

The feeling of disappointment dropped like a stone through my tummy, even though I was well used to these sorts of setbacks. A ship? For five days, according to the ticket, we'd be bobbing around on the North Sea and then the Baltic. I only knew that because of the cities mentioned on the tickets: 'Gottenburg' and 'Helsinki' and 'Leningrad'. Once again my father-assisted geography lessons had come in handy. So here we were in mid-November about to set off across one of the roughest, most exposed stretches of sea in the world. Oh well. At least I'd be missing loads of school . . .

A few days later, I was hanging onto the railing of a broken-down old Soviet cruise ship for dear life as it rocked and rolled over huge sweeping waves while making its way across that very same North Sea. I remember looking across at my mother, wearing a man's sheepskin coat, dark glasses and scarf wrapped over her head. She looked as nonplussed as usual, sitting on a deckchair, staring out into the cloudy distance, puffing on one of her ever present B&Hs. It wasn't exactly a holiday in paradise.

The ship was virtually empty of other passengers, but then who in their right mind would want to go on a Baltic cruise ship in the middle of winter? But none of that bothered my mother. We were on one of her escape routes and I was acting as junior chaperone. And just like so many other occasions in my childhood, I oddly relished the responsibility, which made me feel more grown up. No. Actually it *made* me more grown up. The only thing I'd miss was the chance to slide onto the driver's seat of my mother's Jaguar every day and pretend to drive.

My mum was well aware of that side of my homesickness so she asked the ship's steward if I could go on the bridge to steer the ship every morning. But the stern-looking Soviet captain didn't seem keen.

STEERING THE BIGGEST 'CAR' EVER

He was a big fat man with a beard and he stank of pipe tobacco, and I didn't like the way he kept giving my mother the once-over while he stood just a little too close behind me for comfort as I tentatively tried to steer the ship on the rough open sea.

On the second morning of the cruise, I got so fed up of waiting for my mum to get out of her bed in her cabin (which she had deliberately ensured was down the other end of a long ship's corridor) that I marched back up to the bridge and demanded another go on the huge wooden wheel. This time the captain wasn't there, and a couple of much more friendly merchant sailors even offered me some of their hot chocolate and a bun. I liked it much more up there this time because they didn't mind me being there. I imagined I was the behind the wheel of a massive car. The trouble was you had no sense of being in charge of the ship because it didn't instantly respond to the movement of the wheel, like a normal car.

But at least I wasn't made to feel like an irritant. I lapped up the responsibility of steering the ship. The weather was foul throughout, but that didn't matter. In fact it made it all the more exciting, and I didn't seem to suffer from any seasickness, but then neither did my mother. I think the sailors thought we were a bit odd, though, because they were used to seeing passengers turn green and spend most of their time leaning over the edge depositing their last meal in the sea.

There was definitely an element of risk because the ship was tossing and turning directly into some of the biggest waves I had ever seen in my short life. But the two sailors on the bridge just laughed. Eventually they even showed me how to steer the ship into the really massive waves to avoid rolling the vessel. They laughed along even when the most humungous waves crashed virtually over the top of the bridge, but they clearly wondered what this precocious little kid was doing on the voyage from hell in the first place. I stayed on the bridge that second morning for hours, until the horrible, grumpy captain appeared and I was ordered back down to the main dining area, where my mother was steaming through a very late liquid breakfast at the bar.

She was chatting to a couple of strange-looking men in grey macs while supping a whisky and barely looked up when I appeared. I wished I was still on the bridge steering that huge ship through the waves. I looked the two men up and down suspiciously and went and sat on my own in the opposite corner of the bar.

The next few days followed a very familiar pattern. I'd get up much earlier than my mother. Get irritated because there was nothing much to do and then flick through a few newspapers and comics and go on the bridge. Meanwhile my mum demolished a liquid lunch, followed by a nap in the afternoon, followed by a liquid dinner, followed by a comatose night, before starting all over again the next morning.

We stopped in Helsinki on the way to Leningrad, but I have absolutely no memory of what we did apart from sneaking down the gangplank so I could examine more closely a couple of strange-looking Finnish cars, which I'd never seen before in my life. I don't think we ventured into Helsinki itself. It certainly did not leave an indelible mark on my memory.

But the Soviet Union was altogether a different cup of tea. I remember feeling quite nervous as the ship finally made its way very slowly through the mist into the port of Leningrad, escorted by a very threatening-looking tugboat that kept making 'poop-pooping' sounds. After all, we were now in the 'evil' Soviet Union, where the spies and killers and stuff hung out. This was where they shot people who dared to speak up against the government. The *Daily Mirror*, which I'd read every morning since the age of five, had supplied me with plenty of scare stories down the years.

My take on the Soviets had also been shaped by a lot of tub-thumping on the TV news by the Americans, especially since the Bay of Pigs and the assassination of JFK. My dad had also cranked up the fear factor by referring to how the air-raid shelters from the Second World War might come in handy again if the Soviets decided to drop a nuclear bomb on London. It's odd to think he said all that stuff even though he'd been a Communist in the '30s.

As the ship slowly continued its journey into the port, I watched avidly from the deck. Everything looked grey and bleak and lifeless. There were hardly any people around, except for a few dockworkers and a couple of funny-looking Lada police cars with men wearing hats with enormous patent peaks.

STEERING THE BIGGEST 'CAR' EVER

Across the other side of the port I noticed the Russian battleship the *Aurora* through the mist on the Neva River. It looked very daunting, as if it was there to warn off anyone who approached, while in fact it was just tied up there as a memorial of the Russian Revolution. Although one Englishman next to me on the deck that day insisted its six-inch guns were always loaded 'just in case we tried to invade'. This had been the vessel that had sparked the Bolshevik Revolution of 1912, the same year as my father's birth. The *Aurora* became a symbol for the Russian Revolution when her crew joined the Bolsheviks and refused an order to take to sea – or so the story goes.

My next memory is of an old Volga taxi with squeaking suspension and a nasty-looking red-faced Soviet driver blowing clouds of cigarette smoke out of his mouth. There were Volga taxis everywhere in Leningrad. In fact, there seemed to be few other vehicles. The Volga was probably the ugliest car I had ever seen. I'd noticed from my car books at home that most of the models in the Soviet Union seemed to be named after rivers, which was very apt since this taxi smelled like an open sewer as it slid across the icy blacktop on the way into the city centre.

My mum had been told by a friend back in London that the October Hotel had the finest cocktail bar in the city, so we were en route there in that taxi. I had that familiar feeling of driving trepidation because I didn't like the way this old boy was steering the taxi with one hand and turning round to gesticulate and trying to talk to us while narrowly missing the oncoming traffic.

Eventually we somehow got there in one piece. The October Hotel had a ridiculously ornate bar with a ceiling that must have been 30 feet high and chandeliers the size of giant octopuses. My mother settled in quickly with a vodka martini, and I sat there bored out of my tiny brain. There weren't even many people to watch because the place was as quiet as dew.

Both my mother and I seemed to need some kind of 'fix' of excitement at least once a day. She had her alcohol and pills to water down the lows, but I had nothing but an obsessive curiosity about things. I'd always enjoyed going in lifts because I liked the sensation when they were going down at high speed and you could feel a sort of G-force rush. But on the other hand I did find it quite nerve-racking because there was no driver for a lift, apart from in those really old-fashioned ones where a porter would turn a ratchet to control the movement between floors.

I'd noticed when we'd walked into the October Hotel earlier that the entrances to the three hotel lifts were surrounded in twirly gold leaf, but they did not have porters at attendance. At least that meant no one would notice a nine-year-old kid travelling up and down in them. I kept hearing the *woosh* sound of them while my mother and I sat in the main bar, and since I was bored it seemed to make sense to go on a small adventure. She was on her third vodka martini when I announced that I needed to go to the loo and wandered out of the bar and across the lobby. She didn't even look up from her drink.

A couple of minutes later, I was being transported to the top floor in a creaking old lift accompanied by two elderly men dressed like waiters who squinted straight at me so much that I had to look down to avoid their gaze. I was mightily relieved when we finally reached the top floor because I'd started to convince myself they were Soviet secret police who would probably shoot me for being a foreigner. When the lift doors finally opened, I hotfooted it straight out of there as fast as was humanly possible.

After charging down one enormous, long corridor in the opposite direction to where they had gone, I checked to see if the coast was clear, returned to the lift and pressed the button. After what seemed like an eternity, the creaking double lift doors finally opened. Three expressionless people emerged and walked past without even giving me a second glance. I stepped in and soon I was on my way down, back towards the lobby again. This time, though, we stopped at virtually every one of the twelve floors, and by the time we got to the third, the lift was full of yet more grey middle-aged people, none of whom uttered a word to each other. It felt as if no one under the age of 30 was allowed into the hotel.

Just after the double doors creaked shut on the third floor, I thought I heard an extra clunking noise when the lift started its descent. But no one else seemed bothered so I ignored it, although the lift did seem to be travelling much faster this time.

STEERING THE BIGGEST 'CAR' EVER

A split second later, it shuddered to a halt so suddenly that I was thrown against the cleavage of a plump woman with green teeth and frizzy hair who was standing next to me. I straightened myself up and gave her an apologetic look, but she looked back at me very disapprovingly. Then I realised the lift felt like it was swinging from side to side. It was like being on the end of a pendulum, and my stomach was starting to feel a little queasy.

The other people in the lift said nothing. *Nada.* Not a dicky bird. I was standing next to the floor buttons and wondered for a moment if I had touched one of them by accident and that was why we'd crashed to a halt. The way they all seemed to be looking down at me made me feel it was all *my* fault. Perhaps we were on the second floor and the door was simply being a bit slow to open? No doubt we'd be continuing our journey in a few moments. But, of course, the doors didn't open.

Worse still, every time anyone moved, the lift wobbled in an alarming fashion. I looked up again at all the faces in that lift with me, and this time they all looked away from me and each other. Eye contact was not encouraged. It was as if I was suddenly invisible. I took a deep breath and looked down at the floor, mainly because that was what all the other people were doing. I just presumed someone would take charge and we'd soon be rescued. But this was the Soviet Union in the mid-1960s. Nobody was going to take charge unless they were ordered to do so.

So we just stood there in complete and utter silence. I was a shy kid anyway so I wasn't about to start making polite conversation with any of these miserable, slightly scary-looking people. Worse still, there was now no sound whatsoever coming from anywhere else. Surely there would be some knocking noises or voices? There were only three lifts in the hotel so someone would quickly notice that one of them had stopped working, wouldn't they?

That one woman whose ample cleavage had cushioned my fall earlier was still looking very stern, but I was relieved she was there because the men seemed even scarier. I'd been brought up by my mother and her two sisters while my father was out working long hours at work. I trusted women much more than I trusted men.

CAR TROUBLE

Just then the lift buckled in what felt like mid-air and dropped about a foot, with a huge jolt that nearly knocked us all off our feet. I hung onto the rail around the inside of the lift. For a split second it had felt as if we were about to go into free fall. But yet again no one else in the lift reacted, although the woman with the cleavage did seem to have a slightly concerned look on her face when she glanced down at me. But overall it felt as if the men had been programmed not to say anything.

I slid down into the corner and sat there with my head in my hands, wondering what was going to happen next. I wasn't crying or anything, and even if I had, I don't think any of them would have helped. They'd probably all faced a lot worse than a faulty lift in their lives. I was scared, but it didn't even cross my mind that my mother might be waiting anxiously just two floors below, worried out of her mind about me. I doubted she'd even noticed I was missing. More likely she was on her fourth vodka martini and surrounded by new 'friends'. She probably thought I'd gone for a wander and that I'd be back soon. It was oddly reassuring to think like that because it made things less dramatic if I thought she wasn't worried about me.

Meanwhile the minutes ticked by and still there was not a flicker of emotion on the faces of those people in the lift. I started to wonder if we would ever be rescued. Maybe no one had actually noticed the lift wasn't working? Anything was possible in this strange, inhospitable place. Maybe some of these men were yet more secret police and they would kill anyone under 30 who ventured into the October Hotel?

I don't know how long we stayed there in virtually complete silence, but it seemed like hours and hours. My imagination was running away with me, and I was confused by it all because I couldn't understand why all these people seemed afraid to even speak. I guess it was about an hour later when the lift suddenly sprung into life and we descended to the ground floor.

Not one of those people – including the woman with the cleavage – even said goodbye when the double doors finally creaked open. And, surprise surprise, my mother was not waiting anxiously for my return. I charged off towards the cocktail bar, where I soon spotted her immersed in yet another vodka martini in the company of two very shifty-looking Soviet-spy types in cheap grey suits and nylon shirts.

As I approached, she turned and looked right through me in one of her classic glassy-eyed stares that always meant she was half-cut. I stopped, glanced around and headed to the other side of the bar, where I ordered a lemonade, safe in the knowledge that she hadn't missed me one tiny bit.

DRIVING BACK IN THE REAL WORLD

ONE MORNING BACK IN LONDON A FEW MONTHS LATER, I WAS outside cleaning our beloved British racing green Jag when my mother came tottering down the black-and-white tiled steps of our house. I looked up and noticed she was pulling on her brown-suede-and-beige-crocheted driving gloves. My heart sank because I presumed she was on her way out and I'd be spending the rest of the day on my own, without even the Jag to sit in and pretend to drive.

As I've said before, she was a person of few words so I shut all the open doors I had been cleaning except for the driver's door and stood back and waited for her to drive off in her customary cloud of smoke and a screech of the spoked wheels.

She got in, pulled down her pencil skirt carefully, and then leaned forward, switched on the ignition and pressed the starter button. The Jag roared into life. The strange thing was that her door remained open. She adjusted the rear-view mirror with a quizzical look on her face.

'Hey. Have you been sitting in here again? The mirror has moved.'

I didn't answer her but looked shyly away in the opposite direction, which was my habit whenever I was caught out by her. I'd had enough of feeling awkward so I turned and started to shut her door, but she stopped me.

'Come on. I'm going to give you a proper driving lesson this time.'

Fifteen minutes later and my mother was giving me a driving lesson down a side street near our house. It was like a reward, in a sense, and being out on a *real* road was exhilarating rather than terrifying. I felt grown up, and every time another car passed me it was another notch on my experience of driving. When a Bedford van with sliding doors thanked me for giving way, I was so happy a large knot of excitement fluttered through my stomach. I was a driver just like all those other people in their vehicles.

And there alongside me throughout was my mother. She seemed to have gone into a bit of trance while I was driving. I wondered if that was due to her latest handful of tranquillisers or whether my driving was so good she could genuinely relax. Later I concluded it was probably a bit of both.

Essentially, my mother had put her trust in me and I was doggedly determined not to let her down. She had faith in my driving skills. I'd screwed up every test in class, but here I was doing something that all my schoolmates would have envied. And I just kept thinking to myself, *One day soon I'll have my own car and then I'll be free.*

CORSAIR V4:
A RIGHT LITTLE GOER

ANOTHER WAY THAT MY MOTHER BATTLED WHAT SHE SAW AS the boring and tedious nature of her life was to team up with her two sisters and work as 'exhibition girls' on the stands at the Motor Show, held each year at the Earls Court arena, just a five-minute walk from our home. I have little or no recollection of what their jobs really entailed, but I do remember that it enabled me to get a free pass to the largest collection of brand-new cars in the world.

I'd enter the exhibition hall with them and then I'd peel off, leaving them to go to their strange temporary jobs, trying to persuade punters to buy washing-up liquid for windscreens, stay-fresh cubes that hang off rear-view mirrors and chamois leathers. I'd wander off and head for the brand-new cars, picking up brochures on all of them, which I'd eventually lug home and pore over for weeks and weeks afterwards. And whenever I thought I could get away with it, I'd queue up behind the other visitors at each stand for a chance to sit in the driving seat of everything from a Rolls-Royce Silver Shadow to an Austin A30.

Sometimes the snotty salesmen wouldn't let me behind the wheel on the basis I was just a kid, but most of them seemed to find it amusing to allow a child a few seconds of fantasy driving. Looking back on it, that experience probably later helped me adapt to any car I got in within seconds when it came to driving. Back at the Motor Show, I knew I couldn't start making engine noises like I did at home in my mother's car, so instead I went into my own 'driving bubble' and would swing the steering wheel around a few times and imagine I was out on the real road.

The most memorable 'drive' was when I managed to talk my way into the front seat of a Mercedes 600 Pullman, a vast tank of a limo that was famous for the rock stars – including John Lennon – who owned one of them. I couldn't believe my luck when the elderly gent standing by the front stacked headlights of the 600 smiled down at me and opened the huge, heavy front driver's door and ushered me inside the limo. I'd tried so hard to resist falling in love with the Mercedes because they were German, after all. But my all-time favourite 280SE was a clear descendent of the 600 Pullman, so I couldn't resist it. I'd been brought up on a diet of war comics and surrounded by people who talked about their adventures in the war and their hatred of Germans, but none of it had rubbed off on me. In any case, one of my dad's best friends was a German writer who always gave me more money to spend on toy cars than any other guests at my parents' parties.

At the Motor Show that day I sank into the soft leather upholstery of the 600 and closed my eyes for a moment and imagined gliding through the streets of London in one of the biggest production cars ever manufactured. I remember the soft padded-leather centre of the steering wheel as well as the leather armrest and the vertical speedometer, complete with a huge column gear-change lever. Thank goodness the key wasn't in the ignition because I would have just driven it off there and then.

Eventually I got out very reluctantly when the old-boy salesman pointed out two businessman types waiting to examine the car, and they were probably a little more likely to buy it than me.

So I wandered off, determined as ever to avoid the stand where my mother and aunts were trying their hardest to flash smiles at punters in a bid to flog them the latest car-washing utensils. I stomped right past them through the crowds at one stage without even giving them a second glance because I was so embarrassed. Then I picked up yet more brochures filled with glossy colour photos that I'd take home and then cut out and stick on my bedroom wall.

It was exhausting walking round and round the Motor Show that day, and I was starting to fade a bit when I passed a simulated driving test featuring a maroon Ford Corsair V4. I might have been ten years old, but the urge to try out that simulated ride was burning inside me. I puffed myself up and started queuing behind a bunch of teenage boy-racer types. The idea was to drive the automatic car sufficiently well so as to avoid pedestrians and lamp posts on the route – and then be so impressed by the Corsair that you'd go out and buy one immediately. It was a bit like a flight simulator, and back in the mid-1960s, it seemed pretty radical and futuristic.

By the time it was my turn in the queue, the woman 'hostess' in a red-velvet bikini with a huge black patent-leather belt looked so exhausted by having to deal with us all that I don't think she could be bothered to question how a lone schoolboy could possibly even be considered a potential customer, so she just waved me wearily into the driver's seat.

I noticed a cocky boy in his mid-teens just behind me sneering as I adjusted the rear-view mirror as if this really was the real thing. But then I did already know the correct procedure before setting off in any car – and I didn't give a damn what he thought.

The Corsair had an ice-cold, black, smooth steering wheel, and it felt light from the moment I clamped my hands on it. The simulator then kicked into life with a strange buzzing noise. I held onto it carefully and gently began negotiating the corners at first. It was nice not to have to worry about the gears because it gave me enough time to concentrate entirely on the route the car was taking. As it progressed, I began to gain in confidence. I heard the kid behind me sniggering, but it didn't bother me.

I then pressed harder on the accelerator, and I liked the way the simulator revved more noisily as I increased the speed. The blonde 'hostess' in the ridiculous red-velvet bikini was filing her nails now while waiting for me to finish. I glanced across at the counter and it said '0', which meant I hadn't lost one point by hitting anything throughout the journey so far, which was good. The annoying teenager and a couple of his mates were now studying me more avidly, in complete silence.

I passed the finishing point and an alarm went off with a recorded voice saying: '*You have passed the Corsair test.*' The woman in the red-velvet bikini (I forgot to say earlier that it had tassels on it) leaned across to examine the red flashing light that said 'Pass' 'Pass' 'Pass'.

'Blimey O'Reilly,' she said. 'You passed.'

She pulled out a thick sheet of paper and then rolled it into a long tube and wrapped a bit of string around it. Then she presented it to me. It was my pass certificate for the Corsair V4. I was over the moon. The teenagers looked aghast, and I walked off that stand feeling twice the size I had been when I'd shown up a few minutes earlier. I was very happy to have won something for the first time in my life. I couldn't wait to pin that certificate up on my bedroom wall.

I floated through the crowds at Earls Court and finally made it to the stand where my mother and aunts were working. They were just packing up the last of the chamois leathers. My mother noticed I was looking very pleased with myself and gave me a quizzical glance because usually I looked a bit sad. As usual, my mother didn't pry into why I was happy that day. In some ways I wish she had because then I could have told her about how I'd just passed that driving test. When one of my aunts tried to pull the rolled-up certificate out from under my arm, I refused to let her. It was too late to share my secret with anyone. I'd put it up on my bedroom wall just next to my bed so I could look at it any time of the day or night, without anyone knowing. It was much better to have secrets than tell everyone everything. In any case, knowing something other people didn't know also made me feel grown up.

ROADKILL

BY THE AGE OF II, MY MOTHER WAS REGULARLY GIVING ME illicit driving lessons, mainly in the country lanes near my parents' cottage close to Petersfield, in Hampshire. My mother always did her usual trick of producing a bottle of Dettol that she'd secretly filled with whisky and then sinking into the back seat while I got on with some much needed driving practice. She never barked any instructions about what to do. I'd known what all the Jag switches meant from an early age, and I liked the way she didn't interfere. I'd puff myself up with pride and confidence once I got behind the wheel. It felt like the place I belonged more than anywhere else in the world.

Obviously I preferred real roads because they made me feel more grown up and responsible. I liked reversing back into the entrances of fields and farm tracks just to let people past on narrow lanes. The other motorists always thanked me so profusely. It was nice to be appreciated.

And naturally, the more I drove the more confident I became, and I began putting my foot down more and more, picking up to speeds of 40 and sometimes even 50 miles an hour. And my mother never once told me to slow down. She just sat back and enjoyed enabling me to enjoy myself. It was strange because there weren't really any other examples of that sort of parental nurturing in my life. I guess that's why cars were so important. They bridged that gap. They gave us a common denominator.

But it was inevitable that when a 11-year-old was allowed to drive a 3.4-Litre Mark II Jag, something was going to happen eventually. It all came to a head when I was careering along a very narrow country lane bordered by such high hedges that it was difficult to get any sense of what was happening on the other side of them.

Naturally, I always maintained a high degree of concentration when I was driving. My eyes would snap in all directions. Ahead of me. In the rear-view mirror. Back to the front. Then the side mirrors. I had a circuit in my head, and I made sure I ticked off all the things I should do over and over again. So when I felt something hit the chunky chrome front bumper with a bit of a thud it completely threw me because I hadn't even noticed anything in front of the Jag.

I slammed the brakes on, but remembered just in time that trick I'd learned from my dad's chauffeur about letting my foot off the brake pedal just before it actually stopped to avoid discomfort for passengers. But I obviously didn't do it *that* well because the sudden movement woke my mother, who'd been enjoying an alcohol-fuelled snooze in the back seat after finishing off her customary bottle of 'Dettol'.

'What happened?' she muttered.

I ignored her at first because I was completely freaked out that I might have hit something live.

'What happened?' she repeated, in a very rare hint of impatience.

With the Jag idling, I checked my rear-view mirror and noticed something brown lying still in the middle of the road behind the car. My mother turned and looked at it at precisely the same moment, but, as was so often the case, said nothing.

Then she got out of the Jag and tottered a little unsteadily to where that brown 'thing' was lying. At first I watched her in the rear-view mirror as she poked at it tentatively with the toe of her high heels. She quickly ascertained that whatever it was, it was no longer alive. I remained in the driver's seat, getting more and more nervous about what I'd just run over.

Still watching my mother in the rear-view mirror, I saw her lean down to pick up a limp brown bird that looked a bit like a chicken. I was afraid to get out of the car and face the reality of what I had just done. Then she yelled out, 'Come and give me a hand.' So I reluctantly stepped out and walked obediently round the back of the Jag as my mother approached, holding this dead bird by its neck.

'Yummy. It's a pheasant,' she said with great pride and no shock whatsoever. 'Open the boot.'

I did as I was told, and she flung it in there next to a couple of suitcases we'd brought from the cottage. I was flabbergasted. Why was she keeping this dead animal? Surely we should just put it in the hedge?

'We'll get it plucked and have it for lunch on Sunday,' she said without a hint of irony.

The idea of eating this skinny, hairy creature really bothered me.

My mother was just about to shut the boot when a voice bellowed out: 'You're blocking the road.' We both turned to face a ruddy-faced man with an uncocked shotgun under his arm.

My mother quickly slammed the boot shut and turned back to face our new friend 'Farmer Giles' with one of her classic gap-toothed smiles. But now I wasn't sure whether I should go back in the driver's seat or somehow prompt my tipsy mother in that direction, as she *was* old enough to drive. Typically, she was already one step ahead of me.

'So sorry,' she told the farmer in the most charming, but ever so slightly slurred voice. 'My son is taking driving lessons and we just stopped for him to swap places back with me.'

A huge scowl appeared on his face.

'Driving lessons? Where's the L-plates then?'

I was still shaking, initially from the shock of committing 'roadkill' and now because I thought this farmer might cause us a lot of trouble. My mother looked as nonplussed as ever.

'Oh, I just took them off and put them in the boot,' she said, as casually as if she'd just packed away a bag of shopping.

'You didn't knock down one of my pheasants, did you?' he said, suspiciously squinting his eyes in my direction, as if he was trying to see if I was nervous.

CAR TROUBLE

I looked away shyly just as the farmer's eyes started boring holes in me. My mother rescued me in double-quick time by smiling straight at him, so that he looked away from me.

'They're not in season, you know,' added the farmer, with an evil glint in his eye.

'Oh,' replied my mother.

She had the pheasant plucked at a local butcher's the next day and proudly cooked it for the following Sunday's lunch. It tasted like string and I never wanted to eat game ever again.

AUNT JANET'S CHEVY BEL AIR 'BOAT'

IN KEEPING WITH MY UNCONVENTIONAL CHILDHOOD, IT WAS NO great surprise when my parents decided to pack me off to stay with a relative in New York State in the summer of 1969. The Apollo 11 crew had just landed two men on the moon after taking off from Cape Canaveral, in Florida, so going to America really was quite a big adventure for a twelve-year-old. In any case, I hated the long holidays because I'd often spend days and sometimes weeks cooped up in my top-floor bedroom, sandwiched between all those tenants. I found beaches boring so the traditional holidays weren't all that appealing, either.

My parents were reluctantly obliged to pay an extra fiver on the airfare to New York's Kennedy airport for me to be accompanied on and off the plane by a so-called 'BOAC auntie'. I was totally against the idea of having some strange woman treating me like I was five years old, but my parents were not given a choice by BOAC. In any case, I think I detected a slight hint of anxiety in my mother about sending me on a long journey so far away at such a young age. But then again she wasn't that bothered, otherwise she would never have agreed to send me away in the first place.

CAR TROUBLE

Some of my parents' friends were horrified that they would send a child on his own to such a faraway place. But one of the good things about having such irresponsible parents was that they tended to not give a damn what other people thought.

Don't get me wrong. Going to America was a really Big Deal to me, as it would have been to any 12-year-old. I'd seen the movies and watched the TV shows, and it looked exciting and dangerous out there.

I was dispatched to Heathrow Airport on my two-week holiday in the US of A in a black Ford Consul driven by my father's occasional chauffeur, Eric, who'd earlier taught me some of the driving tricks of his trade. Eric and I had long since formed a bond about cars so I was delighted my mother couldn't be bothered to take me to the airport. I particularly loathed emotional farewells, especially when my mother felt obliged to hug and kiss me in front of other people. So I jumped in up front next to Eric the chauffeur and we soon began talking ten to the dozen about the latest Fords and how my mum should really get my dad's employers to upgrade her Mark II Jag to an S-Type, or wait until the brand-new XJ6s came on the market early the following year.

Eric had a black chauffeur's peak hat, which he always wore when he picked up my father, but I liked the fact he always put it away the moment I jumped in the front of the black Ford Consul. As we drove over the raised section of the M4 on the way to Heathrow that morning, I studied the way he sat in such a relaxed manner at the wheel. He exuded calm, and I always liked that in any driver.

My mother had insisted that I wear a tag on my flannel jacket so the wretched BOAC auntie immediately spotted me when I was dropped at Terminal 1. I can't remember what her name was, but she reminded me of an irritating woman teacher back at my school. She kept calling me 'sonny', which I hated, and when she tried to take me by the hand, I refused, much to her chagrin.

Anyway, after being quickly marched through passport control and into the boarding area, she gave up and left me to my own devices, promising to return when boarding began. For the first time that day I was feeling a little nervous, because I was about to visit a strange country full of gun-toting criminals and I still didn't have a clue who was going to meet me at the other end.

My father had mumbled something about staying with his sister – my aunt Janet – who I had never met and who lived out near the huge Finger Lakes in north New York State. But typically, neither my mother nor father had finalised the arrangements when I departed that morning. Looking back on it, I guess they were trying to shunt me out of the house so they might sort out their ongoing marriage difficulties.

I eventually boarded and found myself on a VC10. They were considered quite glamorous aircraft back in those days, although the rear engines made a hell of a racket on take-off. I do recall that my Coca-Cola went flying when we hit some very nasty turbulence. But I definitely preferred flying on my own because my mother used to dose herself up with dozens of tranquillisers to get through flights, and I hated the way her mouth contorted when she was off her head. It put me off happy pills for life.

On arrival at JFK, I was greeted by another annoying BOAC auntie before I'd even left my seat on the plane, although I was rather relieved to have someone with me because I still didn't know where I was actually going. She told me that my aunt Janet had been in touch with them and that she was meeting me on the other side of customs, which was a relief.

When I finally walked out into the arrivals hall, I got quite a shock. There were people of all sizes, colours and races, and I'd ditched my BOAC auntie by pretending I knew exactly what my aunt looked like, which was a lie. But I didn't want to hold her hand and she'd become quite insistent about it as we'd gone through passport control a few minutes earlier.

Luckily my *real* aunt, Janet, looked a lot like my father and she'd even been sensible enough (she was a teacher by trade, after all) to write 'Wensley Clarkson' in huge letters on a piece of cardboard. I tried to act charming to her, but I found it hard to be instantly nice to strangers, even if they were relatives.

However, my eyes lit up in the parking lot (as they call them in the States) when her car turned out to be an enormous three-year-old Chevrolet Bel Air in metallic green. The front bench seats seemed twice the width of those in my mother's old Zodiac, and this car could not have been more different than the Jag, which had individual bucket seats.

Unfortunately my aunt Janet's driving skills weren't great, especially when she tried to chain-light her cigarettes and took her eye off the road. Aunt Janet was also very short-sighted, and we managed to run a lot of red lights during the seven hours it took to reach her tiny cottage on the edge of Lake Seneca, between Syracuse and Geneseo. By the end of the journey, the car was so thick with cigarette smoke I could barely see out of the windscreen. And Aunt Janet kept banging on about how wonderful the bloody Beatles were. Thank God they were on the verge of breaking up.

I'd never been on one single car journey for so many hours, and the huge lake looked more like a small ocean to me. That night I fought off what seemed like thousands of mosquitoes, and I got up very early on account of the jet lag.

In the morning Aunt Janet announced that she was walking up to the main house, where she was working as a nanny to some millionaire's children. She was a teacher by trade, but had ended up taking a job as a nanny because it included her accommodation, and, as I later discovered, she was on the run from some kind of psychotic ex-husband and preferred to work in low-key jobs.

So there I was, all alone in a strange-smelling little cottage on the edge of the biggest lake I had ever seen in my life. I didn't really know what I was doing there, but since there were no other children to play with, it felt a bit like home in some ways.

Which naturally meant my obsession with driving soon kicked in. So I wandered out of the cottage into the searing, dry August heat and walked around my aunt's Chevy Bel Air. It really was an impressive beast and a half.

I couldn't quite believe the size of it, and I liked the way that Aunt Janet hadn't even bothered to lock it. We were in the sort of place where people left their front doors unlocked at night. I opened the driver's door and just peered inside the car for a few minutes. The Chevy had a huge speedometer the size of a big plate, but, rather disappointingly, it only went up to 120 mph, even though it was armed with a massive V8 that made smaller British cars like a Jag or a Triumph TR3 go like rockets.

That's when I saw the keys in the ignition. I couldn't quite believe my eyes because you'd never leave the keys in a car back in London. It was asking for trouble. I looked around. There was not a soul in sight. But I hesitated because I was in a strange country where they drove on the 'wrong' side of the road and, quite frankly, I was feeling pretty spaced out from the jet lag. Maybe this wasn't such a good idea.

Nah, I corrected myself. *This is too good an opportunity to miss.* I had one last look around and then dived into the driver's side of the vast bench seat. I sat there for a couple of minutes, acclimatising myself to the dashboard, which was remarkably simple, considering the size of the car. But then again, it was probably the equivalent of a Ford Anglia to Americans: a relatively cheap runaround.

Just then I noticed a Lincoln Continental, similar to the one that carried President Kennedy to his death (except this one had a fixed roof), gliding past on a dusty track with picket fences, just fifty yards from the cottage. It must have been Aunt Janet's boss, and it snapped me out of my 'driving mode' just in the nick of time. I watched that Lincoln gracefully sweep up the drive to the main house, where Aunt Janet was looking after the children.

She reappeared just after I'd got into the front bench seat of the Chevy for a second time. She didn't seem at all bothered about me being in the driver's seat. Mind you, I hadn't even attempted to fire up the engine so maybe she just didn't care. She certainly didn't have even a whiff of my dangerous obsession with cars that day, which was probably a very good thing.

A couple of days later, I found myself home alone yet again while my aunt was up looking after the rich kids in the main house. For some weird reason she avoided introducing them to me, although I didn't get on with most other kids at the best of times, so it was no great loss.

So once again I had breakfast on my own and then strolled outside. This so-called holiday was turning out to be even more boring than being with my parents because Aunt Janet seemed to do only three things in life: work, sleep and smoke. We never left the compound in the car throughout those first few days, and I was starting to go a bit stir-crazy.

This time I opened the driver's door of the Chevy and slid straight in without pausing for thought. I felt a lot smaller in this car than anything I had driven in the UK. I started pretending to drive and flicked the automatic column gear-change lever up and down and then left it on 'N' for Neutral. Suddenly the Chevy lurched forward and started rolling down the hill. I held on tighter to the wheel and pressed down gently on the brake, expecting it to stop, but it kept going.

The Chevy was soon heading straight down the hill that separated the cottage from the water. I was starting to panic by this stage. No amount of stamping on the brake seemed to do anything to stop the Chevy heading straight for the short pier at the end of the field in front of my aunt's cottage. I couldn't understand what was happening. None of the switches on the dash seemed to respond when I started flicking them all on and off frantically in the hope that something might stop the car. The Chevy was rolling over bumps in the field and picking up speed at an alarming rate.

All I could see in front of me was the blue water of the lake.

I noticed my aunt in the distance to my right. She was running down the hill towards me with two men on either side of her, but I feared they'd never get to the Chevy in time.

I prayed that the brakes would suddenly work and I could stop it. I virtually stood up and with my right foot stamped hard on the brake pedal, but it did nothing to slow the car down. I heard my aunt yelling in the distance just as the Chevy mounted the loose wooden boards of the jetty, still gaining speed.

Next thing I knew, the front tyres of the car got caught in a gap in the planks on the wooden jetty and the Chevy stopped with an almighty jerking movement.

Aunt Janet was not even annoyed with me and rather sweetly blamed herself for leaving the car unlocked on a hill. I think she was just relieved that nothing serious had happened to either me or the car, and she asked me not to mention the incident to my parents, which I was more than happy about.

But that incident did teach me a huge lesson. I decided it was a bad omen and I wouldn't try to 'test out' any cars on this trip because I had a feeling it might turn out to be more trouble than it was worth.

A MINI COOPER ON THE LAM

I'D ALWAYS HAD A SOFT SPOT FOR THE MONTE CARLO RALLY. I'D recreated it on my bedroom floor dozens of times since I was about five years old. I had a mini Scalextric set with rally Mini Coopers, and I had Corgi versions as well, and I often mixed them all up and added extra tracks with imaginary ravines and mountains, made out of cardboard.

But when *The Italian Job* starring Michael Caine came out in cinemas in 1969, that refuelled my obsession to drive a Mini Cooper for real. So I worked very hard to try to persuade Kevin – one of my few friends – that it would be fine to borrow his mother's bright-red Mini Cooper while she was away one weekend. I was 13 at the time.

That's how I came to be round at Kevin's house, trying to help him track down his mum's car keys so we could have a bit of fun. Kevin seemed a tad reluctant at first. But I was determined to get him to do it. Then a broad smile came over his freckly face and he produced the keys from his pocket. He'd been pulling my leg and was really just as keen as me. I'd had a plan inside my head for ages to do something really crazy if we managed to get hold of the Mini Cooper. I wanted to replicate *The Italian Job*. I hadn't told Kevin or anyone else what I had up my sleeve, and I'd decided not to say a word until we were actually out in the Mini.

CAR TROUBLE

I was almost six feet tall by this time so the Mini seemed a bit pokey, putting it mildly. I was more used to the relative space and luxury of Jags and Zodiacs and Chevy Bel Airs. But I found it surprisingly easy to handle the gear and clutch coordination, considering I usually drove automatics.

Initially, Kevin seemed quite relaxed next to me as we set off from his house that Sunday evening. I kept my speed modest on the built-up roads because we certainly didn't want to get stopped by the police. In any case, I had a plan, which involved cranking up the gears and having some outrageous fun, so I didn't want to spoil that.

My favourite scene in *The Italian Job* was when the cars were driven down hundreds of steps in Milan. It's a wonderful part of the film, and I know for a fact that it really did happen and nothing was faked. I wanted to do my own special version of it. But I wasn't mentioning any of this to Kevin quite yet because I didn't want to worry him.

However, he did soon point out we were driving in the direction of our school. I told him not to fret about it, but he didn't look too impressed with my comment.

About half a mile from the gates to our school, I swung into the entrance of a caravan park that ran alongside the border of the college grounds. Kevin had gone very quiet by this stage. Meanwhile, I was just getting into my stride.

It was about nine o'clock on a Sunday evening, and I knew all the boarders at my school would soon be tucked up in bed by now, so there wouldn't be anyone wandering around who we might 'bump' into, in every sense of the word.

I stopped the Mini Cooper in front of a gated back entrance to the school and got out and unbolted it. Kevin still looked far from happy, but he couldn't exactly abandon me because I was driving his mother's car. I got back in and revved the car up as a clear message of intent to him, even though it was a reckless thing to do because it risked 'announcing' our arrival. He still didn't know what I was planning, and from the look on his face, I'd say that he might not have wanted to know.

'Put your seat belt on,' I said.

Kevin didn't ask why. He just did it.

I revved up the engine a second time, closed down the headlights and took off, with a spin of the front wheels in the mud.

I knew I only had a small window of time to do what I had wanted to do for years. I raced along the muddy track between the trees in the wood on the north-eastern corner of the school grounds. I only had my sidelights on because I still wanted to take everyone by surprise. At last Kevin piped up: 'What the hell are you doing? We're going to be shot if we get caught doing this.'

'Doing what?' I felt like saying to him because he didn't even know what I had in store, yet. But then again, he knew me well enough to realise that whatever it was, it would cause a big bang, in every sense of the expression.

We emerged from the wood onto the grass of one of the smaller rugby pitches. The Mini gripped the surface very well, considering it was damp that night. I decided to take the car right along the full length of the field because my 'target' was at the other end.

Kevin was hanging onto the overhead handle above his door for dear life now and seemed frightened to speak. I must have had a determined, detached look on my face because I was so focused on what I was doing that I started not really caring what he was feeling like. I was on a mission.

I picked up more speed as we continued heading across the rugby pitch because I knew we would need it to mount the bank of grass at the other side. As we approached the bank, I turned the Mini Cooper so that I could hit it at an angle, which would hopefully reduce the impact of the steepness and enable me to reach the point above the bank that I was aiming for.

Kevin gasped as we seared through the grass, and I double declutched when we hit the bank to try to help us climb more rapidly. But all I managed to do was create a lot of wheelspin, which knocked us off course, and we slipped back down the bank with a bit of a thud.

I turned the Mini Cooper round so the nose was this time facing directly in front of the grass bank, and shoved her into first and then second gear in fast succession in the hope this might do the trick.

It worked. We climbed the bank at high speed and then landed on the flat surface of the tarmacked athletics track above it, just as

I had planned. I straightened the Mini out and reversed it to the track's starting line, where Kevin and I had struggled in so many lousy athletics events in the past.

I began revving the Mini Cooper really loudly because I knew we'd be seen and I thought it was time to announce our arrival. The Mini Cooper screeched loudly as we took off like lightning, with tyres burning.

I knew I only had five minutes at the most before a load of staff priests appeared on the scene, followed shortly after by the police. But I still managed to tear round the athletics track without a care in the world. I noticed some kids leaning out of their dormitory windows, watching us avidly from the main building of the school.

That's when Kevin started getting really into it. He was screaming his head off as we careered around each curve of the track. The smell of burning rubber on the tarmac was filling the air in a very reassuring way. I did two more noisy circuits of the track and then noticed a couple of fat priests in cassocks struggling through the muddy grass on the ground level between the athletics track and the main school building.

It was time to make an exit, but this could be even trickier than getting up the steep bank. I didn't have time to ponder on which angle to use to get off the track, so I pulled the steering wheel to the left and crossed my fingers. The Mini began sliding down the bank at a precarious angle, and I was seriously worried that the entire vehicle might topple over.

It eventually skidded down the slopes to the ground level below with a bit of thump but no damage. I revved up again, just as the two priests were struggling up the grassy bank that led down to the main school building.

We shot off in the opposite direction, back towards that same rugby pitch from earlier, and I decided to drive the Mini between the two rugby posts just to show off. Kevin was having kittens as I raced towards the posts. He then covered his eyes with his hands. I didn't blame him because I wasn't entirely sure if they were wide enough apart for us to get through.

I steered the wheel dead centre so the Mini was heading straight between the posts and hoped for the best. As we got closer to the posts, they seemed to get smaller. For some weird reason I felt the urge to drive even faster, so I put my foot down harder and the Mini picked up even more speed.

Then I checked my rear-view one last time. If we got stuck between those posts, we were in trouble in more ways than one. I counted down to the rugby posts out loud, just to wind up Kevin, who was cowering with his legs up on the seat as we approached them.

'Ten, Nine, Eight, Seven, Six, Five, Four, Three, Two, ONE!'

He then opened his eyes, but we were already through. Not even the wing mirrors had been clipped. I flicked on the full headlights and steered the Mini towards the far corner of the rugby pitch, where the track through the woods began.

Kevin was laughing his head off despite having been close to tears just a minute earlier. We were back at his house within 15 minutes, but he made me promise we would never try a stunt like that ever again.

No one ever worked out it was us who did the *Italian Job* raid on the school, but it was talked about for years afterwards. Kevin and I had a right laugh examining the skid marks the next morning. At one stage, a rumour went round the school that it had been us, but that was soon quashed by our constant denials. I told Kevin, 'Just deny it until you're blue in the face. They don't have any proof, and that's all that matters.'

He did as he was told, and we had the satisfaction of knowing we'd got away with an outrageous stunt, *and* Kev's mum got her Mini Cooper back without realising it had even left the garage.

A 'LEMON' ON FOUR WHEELS

THE DAY MY MOTHER AND I WAVED FAREWELL TO OUR BELOVED British racing green 3.4-Litre Mark II Jag was one of the saddest days of my childhood. After all, this was the car that had helped launch my driving 'career'. I knew virtually every crease on its olive-green leather upholstery. I adored the way the switches on the dashboard flicked downwards. I liked the Jaguar badge on the steering wheel, not to mention the silver jaguar on the bonnet. But most of all, I loved the spark of power that surged through into the engine when I pressed the starter button.

The Jag oozed class and it turned heads, especially with my eccentric mum and her peroxide-blonde hairstyle at the wheel. The sight of women driving such macho cars was still unusual back in those days. But my mother had decided she was bored of the Jag and wanted something a little *different*. How was I to know she'd decided on a ghastly vomit-beige Citroen DS19 Pallas? It was named after a lemon and it was as ugly as one. On the day it showed up outside our house, I cringed and ran straight up to my bedroom and couldn't even face looking out of the window at it.

But my mother saw this huge, bulbous creature as a long overdue return to her French 'roots'. I'd rather have crawled to my horrible school on my hands and knees than be seen in that embarrassing, sluggish *lemon*. When my mother donned her brown-suede-and-beige-crocheted driving gloves and announced we were going to drive up Kensington High Street in it, I only agreed to go because I wanted to study how to drive it. I was outside our house when I noticed the front doors opened in the opposite direction from any other car in the world at that time. I went right off it even more.

We moved sluggishly through the streets near our house in the Citroen and my mother ended up in a quiet tree-lined street off Kensington High Street. She wanted to 'get the hang of it'. I don't honestly know why she bothered. After one three-point turn that ended up taking at least twenty points to complete, my mother decided to test out the pneumatic suspension for what seemed like hours. It was soon making me feel a lot more seasick than that five-day cruise across the North Sea *and* the Baltic. I also hated the way the gear stick stuck out from the dashboard and looked as if it was much harder to use than a traditional column or stick shift. I wanted my mother to have a car I could just get into and drive. Not some weird-looking vehicle with front headlights that made it look like an ugly giant frog (and that's not a play on words with the French).

A few days later, my mother went off with my father to a party in the West End, and I clambered into the Citroen to try to give it a 'test drive'. I'd studied my mother's driving skills enough to believe I could handle the car, but I got the shock of my life when the pneumatic suspension began rising after I switched on the ignition. That suspension was about as useful as a snooze button on a smoke alarm. It really was an alien spaceship compared to the good old Jag. Having started the engine I sat there and tried to decide what to do next, before turning it off and retreating back to my bedroom.

For the following few months, I steadfastly refused most offers of a ride in the Citroen because I felt so embarrassed to be seen out anywhere in it. Luckily my mother quickly lost patience with it too, as it kept breaking down virtually every week. The repair bills were astronomical because the spares had to be shipped over from France. And I have felt a grudge against Citroens ever since.

HITTING TOWN IN A BRAND-NEW MOTOR

STRANGELY ENOUGH, MY MOTHER SEEMED TO OFTEN END UP WITH cars that the police used, which suited me because I liked imagining I was a policeman, since they got to drive faster than anyone else. I'm not including the dreaded Citroen, of course, although come to think of it there were police versions across the Channel. But there had been the Zodiac (as used in TV's *Z-Cars* and real life), the Jag (everywhere on telly and in real life) and now she was about to take delivery of a Triumph 2000 Mark II. My mother obviously liked taking people by surprise, and seeing a middle-aged peroxide blonde speeding down the street in something the police usually drove certainly turned a few heads.

Our new Triumph 2000 was even white – the same colour as most police cars at the time. It was also an automatic, which meant it would be a doddle to drive compared to the stupid Citroen and its weird gear stick and irritating up-and-down suspension. I was already (in my own mind, at least) an accomplished driver. I was tall and could easily pass for 16 or 17, so I now had the confidence to pull off acting older than I really was.

Within hours of my mother taking delivery of that gleaming, immaculate, brand-new white Triumph 2000 automatic, I'd decided to find the perfect opportunity to 'borrow' it. So I took every driving trip out with my mother that was on offer in an effort to educate myself about the switches and how best to handle the Triumph. I liked its sleek Italian lines and the double horizontal headlights and the narrow grille that provided the Triumph with a unique 'face' all of its own. It was a sneaky expression, almost as if the Triumph was squinting at everyone, examining them in minute detail.

Not long after we got the Triumph, my mum and dad stopped at a pub for a drink and left me outside in the car as usual. They could have taken me into pubs by this time because I looked much older than my real age, but I didn't encourage it because I much preferred being in my own little motoring netherworld than making awkward conversation while they knocked back double gins at a rate of knots.

So that afternoon in the pub car park, I nipped into the front seat and tried the Triumph's steering wheel for size. Then I tested the switches out in preparation for my debut drive, which I hoped would happen very soon. Eventually my parents rolled out of the pub to find me in the front seat, and my dad laughed and made a joke about how I was 'a bit young to drive yet'. Then I caught my mother's eye and she put her forefinger to her lips. I smiled. All those previous 'driving lessons' were our little secret. As I've mentioned, we both liked having secrets.

That afternoon we almost had a serious crash on Hammersmith Bridge when my mum lost concentration and swerved in front of a Number 73 bus. My dad was so shocked by our near miss that he actually lost his temper, which was very rare for him. He and my mother bickered all the way home, and I put my hands over my ears to drown it out, but as usual I still heard every word. Outside our house she crunched the Triumph into reverse to back her into the carport, still arguing, and nearly ended up reversing into the front window of the basement, where yet another tenant lived. But she eventually agreed with my dad not to drive to a party they'd been asked to the following night.

At times like this it often felt like I was invisible, in a sense, because my parents would enter their own little world of domestic 'unbliss' and seemed to forget I was even there. But I was more interested in knowing they would both be out because that sounded like a perfect opportunity for me to 'test drive' the Triumph.

The following day, I waved goodbye to my mother from the bay window of the sitting room as she got in the back of a black cab on her way to meet my father. She was dressed head to toe in Chanel. I knew they were going to be out for the rest of the day and most of the evening because I'd dragged the information out of my mother that morning over breakfast.

She must have wondered why I was being so chatty because we rarely had those sorts of inane conversations. I remember catching my mum looking at me in a rather quizzical manner, with her head slightly tilted to one side. I'm sure she had a sneaking suspicion of what I was up to, but she did nothing to dissuade me. That just wasn't her style. I'd like to think she was giving me her tacit approval, in a sense. She certainly knew I was an only child who needed an outlet and cars had become that outlet. As far as I was concerned, they more than made up for not having many friends.

Anyway. That afternoon, I waited a few minutes just in case my mother came back, having forgotten something, and then slipped upstairs to my parents' bedroom and opened the small cupboard above the chest of drawers, where I knew she always kept the spare key to her car. I reached up to it and stopped for a split second, wondering if I should be about to do this – steal my mother's new car. But that feeling passed in a nanosecond. I snatched the key off the hook, dropped it into my trouser pocket, headed out of the bedroom door and bumped straight into Miss Hogg, our elderly tenant who often fed me when my mum was sleeping off a hangover or out for a late night. I looked up and smiled, and then she said the words I had dreaded: 'I've just bought some really nice digestives. They'd go down a treat with some hot chocolate. Why don't you pop up?'

Miss Hogg had been my surrogate grandmother since I was three years old, and she'd been having increasing problems appreciating that I was now a teenager. I smiled back politely and mumbled something about having to go out to see a friend, which was half true, since I was planning to go out. She looked mortified and shuffled off up the stairs with her shopping. Like most of the women in my childhood she seemed to have a sixth sense about things, and I would swear she knew what I was up to. But on the other hand, I probably sensed that purely because I felt a bit guilty about letting her down. Mind you, I felt guilty about letting *anyone* down.

I was quite agitated by the time Miss Hogg disappeared because I felt that every interruption was delaying my road trip, and I knew I only had a short window of time. I dashed down the stairs two at a time, grabbed a front-door key off the hall table and headed out the door.

The Triumph 2000 looked huge sitting out in the carport in front of our house, and I gulped for a moment because it seemed much more daunting than the smaller Jag. But there was no time for second thoughts. I was already on a 'high' from the excitement and there was no way I would – or could – change my mind.

By this time my hands were shaking so badly that I struggled to get the key in the driver's door lock. At first it didn't seem to fit, and I got into a bit of a panic. Why wouldn't it work? I nearly snapped it off with irritation. Maybe I had the wrong key? Then I pulled it out and realised it was upside down. I pushed it back in and, hey presto, it slid straight in and the button inside popped up as the lock connected. I was in.

It was lucky my mother had reversed the Triumph into the carport the previous day after that close shave with the Number 73 bus on Hammersmith Bridge, because I'm not sure I could have coped with reversing out into a busy London street.

I turned the ignition key firmly and got quite a scare because the engine fired up instantly. I'd been more used to the Jag, which had a starter button that often took ages to spark the engine into life. I sat there frozen to the seat for a few moments. This was a brand-new car and I was running the risk of ruining it. Kevin's mum's Mini Cooper had felt much less daunting in a strange way. Then I looked around to see if anyone was watching me. It was a natural instinct because we had five tenants living in the house on the top floor and in the basement at the time, so I wanted to make sure none of them spotted me.

I let the handbrake off and waited for the Triumph to creep forward, but it stood completely still. I was thrown for a moment. Then I looked down at the stick shift automatic lever and realised the car was still in 'P' for Park. I slid the lever very quickly through to 'D' for Drive, afraid that if I did it too slowly the car might stop in 'R' for Reverse and end up with the boot going through the window of one of the basement's bedsits.

The Triumph surged forward, so I braked hard and it jerked to a halt halfway across the pavement in front of the carport. I sat there for about a minute, wondering if I really had the guts to go through with this. I waved to an old lady waiting to walk across in front of me on the pavement. That gave me a bit more confidence.

I adjusted the rear-view mirror, looked left to make sure nothing was coming, took my foot gingerly off the big brake pedal and stroked the accelerator. The Triumph dipped down slowly into the kerb and then up again. The entire process was taking too long and a pack of cars was certain to appear from the other end of the street if I didn't hurry up. So I banged my foot down harder on the accelerator and the Triumph's bonnet surged up and I swung the steering wheel to the right and within seconds I was driving in the road itself.

I'd done it. I was out on my own and no one had stopped me. I was gliding along when I heard a furious hooting sound from behind me. I looked in the rear-view and what seemed like half a dozen cars were right up close behind me. I knew I had to go faster or else they'd wonder what the hell I was doing, and that meant there was a danger I would get stopped by the police.

I pressed down harder on the accelerator and the Triumph picked up speed at the same time as I picked up yet more confidence. I checked my rear-view carefully again and then allowed my eyes to snap around in front of me. Ooooops. Traffic lights ahead. They were just going amber so I let my foot off the accelerator and pressed hard on the brake pedal. The Triumph almost stopped dead, but then I remembered that old trick shown to me by the chauffeur and let my foot off the pedal momentarily so that I glided to a halt at the lights.

I even allowed myself the luxury of leaning my elbow on the window edge of the door and turning up the wireless to listen to the chart show on Radio 1. I glanced across and looked at the driver next to me, an old boy in a Rover 2000 sucking on a pipe and wearing a tweed trilby. He looked across enviously. He nodded while examining my brand-new Triumph 2000. It was the latest version so it was only natural that other motorists would be interested. I was in the real driving world and it felt really great, and naturally I beat the old boy hands down when the lights went green.

The difference now was that I was confident and in control of my own destiny. I took the next right into Earls Court Road and decided to head down the A4 towards Heathrow Airport. I soon found myself on a dual carriageway, something I had never driven on before. I'd always wondered how you kept inside your lane without drifting, but it was surprisingly easy. *Everything* felt easy.

I kept the Triumph at a steady 60 mph once I was settled on the A4, but I noticed a lot of traffic was passing me so I decided to take her up to 70 mph. Butterflies in my tummy kicked in when I looked at the speedometer and the needle hovered just over the 80 mph mark. My eyes were transfixed by that '80'. I felt almost invincible, in a sense. It was a nice feeling. I kept the Triumph steadily at that speed as the road curved out towards Heathrow Airport, and then I slowed down and took the next roundabout in order to head back to London.

Soon I was back up at 80 mph, but I couldn't seem to stop myself admiring the needle on the speedometer. *I was driving at 80 miles an hour.* I was so proud of what I was doing that I needed the reassurance of seeing what speed I was driving at. It was really happening. I wasn't imagining it.

But maybe I kept my eye on that speedometer just a little too much, because suddenly I was being hooted at. I looked behind me and a carload of men was right up my arse, as they say in the world of motoring. I was a bit panicked, but I just decided to keep driving at the same speed. Maybe I should have moved over, but no one had taught me what you were supposed to do in such circumstances.

The next blast of the hooter was continual and much more aggressive. They were even closer behind me, but the dual carriageway was so crowded I couldn't move over to let them past. I looked in my rear-view mirror again and this time I noticed the driver swigging on a bottle of something. They were drunk. Not good.

I was afraid of speeding up in case I attracted the attention of the police. But I was also very scared of the men behind me. Every time I looked in the rear-view I could see the aggression in their faces, and they were incredibly close to the back of the Triumph.

I'd long since stopped glancing at the speedometer in case it distracted me from the road ahead in any way. So I kept my eyes focused ahead and tried to block the drunks behind me out of my mind. But they made sure that didn't happen by regularly blasting me with their hooter. I just couldn't make up my mind whether to swing across into the other lane and risk a crash or keep driving with these bastards up my backside.

Eventually, I checked out the traffic carefully enough to finally swing across into the slow lane. I was so relieved that I allowed the Triumph to slow down to a respectable 50 mph and hoped that would be the end of their tailgating.

But within seconds their hooter went off again. I glanced nervously in my rear-view mirror and there they were, right behind me. They'd moved over to the slow lane and were now trying to intimidate me by virtually touching bumpers. They were so close I could now see the ruddy complexions of the two in front and they also had the most horrible grins on their faces.

I was melting down fast because I didn't really know what to do and these bastards were determined not to let go of me. Luckily I knew the road quite well from having been out many times with my mother, so I decided to exit the dual carriageway at Hammersmith roundabout and then head up towards where I lived. I didn't know what else to do.

I was dreading any traffic lights because I knew that if I stopped then these drunks would probably pile out and get me. I wasn't worried about my own safety. I just wanted to make sure I got the Triumph home in one piece without anyone knowing what I'd been up to, because I didn't want to lose any chance of doing this in the future.

Then I remembered something from a few months earlier when my mum had been hauled into a police station after she'd clipped another car and not bothered stopping to exchange details. I'd been left outside that police station for ages in our car while she talked her way out of trouble as usual.

That afternoon the only traffic lights on Hammersmith Broadway were green, thank God, and as I circled the roundabout, I decided to swerve left instead of heading in the direction of my home because the last thing I wanted was this lot attacking me in front of my own house.

I checked my rear-view and they were still there, hooting away almost constantly and sometimes hollering at me out of the windows. I just prayed that my little plan might work. About 200 yards up Shepherd's Bush Road I slammed on my brakes and slithered to a halt by the side of the road. The idiots behind me did likewise.

I locked the doors and sat there and waited for them to come and get me. Two of the men ran to the front of the Triumph and started banging on the window for me to get out. It was vicious, intimidating stuff, and remember, I was just 13 years old. I tried to ignore them, but then they started banging so hard on the window that I was afraid it might break.

That's when I finally looked one of them straight in the eye and pointed behind him to the blue light hanging outside the small building just ten yards from where he was standing. We were outside Hammersmith Police Station. The drunk stopped in his tracks, turned and looked at the blue light, then grabbed his mate and rushed back to their car and they drove off at high speed.

I sat there for a couple of minutes, shaking like a leaf. Suddenly there was a tap on the window, which made me jump. I looked up and it was a uniformed copper. Shit. I was going to get nicked and it was all my fault. The copper was telling me to wind the window down. I took a long gulp and then slowly unwound it. 'You're on a double yellow, son.' I nodded very slowly and tried to smile, and then I wound up the window again, took a long, deep breath, let the handbrake off, flicked on the indicator and pushed the automatic gear lever back into 'D' for Drive.

Ten minutes later, I ever so carefully reversed back into the carport in front of my family home and even checked to make sure it was in the exact same spot it had been before I had stolen it two hours earlier. I just hoped my mother wouldn't notice the change in the fuel gauge. But I doubted that she ever worried much about such things.

I was just flipping the car key back onto its hook in the bedroom cupboard when I heard my parents stumble into the hallway below . . . It had been quite an adventurous day, and getting away with it had made it even more exciting.

FUELLING AN OBSESSION . . .

I STOLE MY MOTHER'S TRIUMPH REGULARLY. I CALLED IT 'borrowing' earlier, but what's the point of beating about the bush? I stole it. There is no other accurate way to describe it. I even devised a way of making enough cash to replenish the petrol whenever I took the car out on any particularly long journeys.

I'd always been well aware of my mother's virtually non-stop consumption of Tuinal tranquillisers, which GPs seemed to hand out like sweets back in the 1950s and 1960s. I used to stumble upon numerous half-empty little bottles of them all over the house, and I'd often hide them or even throw them away because I hated the way she relied on them so heavily.

But now I was 13 and looked old enough to go in pubs, and I'd got to know a group of teenagers who were unconnected to my school, which was probably why they were friends with me in the first place. Most of them were at least two or three years older than me and they were always banging on about drugs.

So one day I slipped one of my mother's half-empty bottles of Tuinal into my pocket and produced them in the pub with my mates. Perhaps not so surprisingly, one of the other boys revealed that his own mum was on Tuinal when he read the label on the bottle. He said he'd tried one with a pint of beer once and it worked rather well. I didn't really have a clue what he meant.

So I spread ten Tuinal out in front of me on the table in the pub and flogged eight of them for 10p each. That gave me enough money for a few pints and something left over to use as petrol money the next time I took my mother's Triumph.

I also began putting a few bob aside in a secret stash in my bedroom because I wanted to buy my own car one day, and I certainly wasn't going to wait until I was legally old enough to drive, either. There were many occasions when I thought my mum would be sure to spot that some of her 'happy pills' were missing, but she never even bothered to ask me. I actually think she had so many bottles of them stashed around the place that she'd long since lost track of what she actually had. If she did ever find out, I think she might have been under the impression that I was taking them, rather than selling them. But her head was fogged up so much of the time that none of it seemed to really matter to her.

TRIUMPH WITH A GIRL IN A PINK COAT

BY THE TIME I WAS ABOUT 13 AND A HALF, I WAS TAKING THE Triumph out for secret driving trips virtually every week, especially during the school holidays. It tended to be in the evenings when my parents were out so I got used to night driving from a very early age.

But taking the Triumph out for a spin on my own was starting to lose its appeal. I wanted to be with other people when I was driving it. I was proud of my skills behind the wheel. I felt the same age as my new set of friends, who were 15 or 16 and in some cases 17. *And none of them could drive or had access to a car.*

One day I called up directory enquiries to find out a number for a toy-model shop that I wanted to visit and I got talking to the woman operator, who had a very nice voice. We completely engaged with each other on the phone and I ended up talking to her for about half an hour. She asked me how old I was and I said '17'. It seemed a natural enough response.

The following night my parents were out at yet another drunken bash, and I was driving over Battersea Bridge for a blind date with the girl from directory enquiries. It was my first date and I was extremely nervous. She'd sounded very nice and easy-going on the phone and said she'd be standing outside Clapham South Northern Line tube station in a pink coat so I'd easily spot her. I didn't give much thought to what was happening, really. I was just swept up with the idea that a girl – older than me – liked me enough to agree a date. She'd think I was 17 because I'd be in my own car.

I was relishing the idea of being out with a girl in a flash car. I was sure it would impress her and that couldn't be a bad thing. The only problem with picking her up in Clapham was that I had no idea where it was because it was that dreaded area known to people round where I lived as 'south of the river'.

So. Armed with an A-Z of London, I'd set off early from Kensington and allowed an hour to get to Clapham, which was only about three miles away. I kept having to grab the A-Z from the passenger seat next to me and it took me half an hour just to get to Battersea Bridge, which wasn't a good start, but I soldiered on. I'd conquered most aspects of driving, but trying to read the A-Z and drive at the same time wasn't always easy. But I was determined not to let this girl down and, in any case, she must have been at least 16 to have that job as an operator for directory enquiries.

I eventually found my way through Battersea and up to Clapham before getting caught up in a huge one-way system round the Common. I was in danger of running late and, thanks to my flaky mother, I had an almost pathological obsession with being punctual.

Running late was making me much more nervous than the driving, which I always thoroughly enjoyed. I finally cracked the stupid one-way system round Clapham Common and headed along the side towards Clapham South tube station. It was dark and raining, and the streets this far south of the river didn't seem as well lit as they were round where I lived.

Spotting a girl in a bright pink coat wouldn't be that hard, surely? I turned and scanned the entrance to the tube station, but there was no one there, so I headed round the block to come back in a couple of minutes.

I didn't want to stop in the middle of the street anyway, so I kept on driving, knowing I'd be back outside the tube station again very shortly. This time I tried to slow down a bit more and risked the anger of other drivers because I was worried that I might have missed her, even though I was still more or less on time.

That's when I saw her and put my foot down on the accelerator. She caught my eye as I drove past so I knew it had to be her. I looked away, desperate to avoid her gaze. I'd seen enough. She looked about 40, but worse still, her bright-pink coat was wrapped around a body that must have weighed at least 30 stone, which was why I spotted her so easily.

I felt so bad about letting her down that I stopped the car round the corner to try to compose myself. I took a few deep breaths and then checked the rear-view before heading off again, and there she was coming towards me. She'd obviously worked out it was me from my description on the phone.

I slammed my foot down hard on the gas pedal and nearly hit a Morris Minor – which I had not even noticed – as I pulled away. No doubt she knew it was me because I'd told her I had a white Triumph 2000. But she represented one dose of grown-up reality I was not yet ready to face.

I drove straight home that evening and decided never to call telephone directory enquiries ever again. I'd stick to the phone book. Much safer.

A CRAWLING BEETLE
IN PUTNEY

CARS WERE, IN A SENSE, AN EXTENSION OF MY PERSONALITY.
I lived my life through them. I dreamed about them when I was
asleep and daydreamed about them when I was awake. Even my
hormones seemed to be connected to cars – look at the way I'd used
my mother's Triumph to set up that blind date.

But that disastrous non-encounter with a member of the opposite
sex didn't stop me being convinced that the only way I would get a
girlfriend was to pretend to be older than I was and make sure I had
a car to impress her with. The trouble was that at almost 14 my access
to cars was restricted to 'borrowing' the Triumph or nicking a friend's
parents' vehicle. And after that escapade with Kevin on the school
athletics track, my few friends didn't seem keen on helping me steal
their parents' motors.

However, my mate Jamie turned out to be one exception to
that rule. He'd listened with fascination as I'd told him about my
adventures in my mother's car and made it clear he'd be up for
some similar escapades. So one day I was sitting round his kitchen
table demolishing a tin of cold baked beans when we decided that it
might be fun to 'borrow' his mum's bright-orange VW Beetle, since

she was away on holiday in Cornwall at the time.

Jamie was a game sort of bloke who was up for virtually anything, especially after a drink or two, or something stronger. He was a wiry kid, but as hard as nails. The sort of person you always wanted on your side in a fight.

Anyway, we were sat there in his kitchen in Putney when he pulled the VW keys out of his pocket and dangled them in front of me. 'But there's one condition,' he said, with a wry smile on his face.

I shrugged my shoulders. 'Sure.'

'I get to drive some of the way.'

Having a co-driver was something I hadn't even considered, and it did leave me a little worried because I knew how hard it was to just get in a car and drive for the first time. I'd done it when I was eight years old. I didn't really fancy risking life and limb with a rookie driver, and although Jamie was a game sort of bloke, he also had a very nervy side to him. I had a feeling he wouldn't turn out to be a natural driver. Now, you may ask how I, aged fourteen, could even have a clue what a 'natural driver' was, but there are definitely two distinct types of motorists out there: the ones who know instinctively what they are doing and the ones who don't have a clue. The trouble is if you're one of the former then it's quite scary being driven by one of the latter. Think about it.

Anyway, I put all that into the back of my mind while Jamie called up a couple of girls he knew in Guildford and arranged to meet them in a pub later that day. Ten minutes later Jamie and I were sitting in the Beetle, trying to get it to start without much success. We checked the petrol gauge and there seemed to be plenty in it, but the bloody thing just wouldn't spark into life.

Eventually Jamie and I decided the only solution was to push the Beetle out of the lock-up and try to bump-start her. Luckily, I knew how to bump-start cars because I'd helped my aunt push her VW estate when I was working for her at Portobello Market one afternoon. It was a risky strategy because some of the neighbours in his street might spot us, and they'd be sure to tell his mum when she got back from her holiday. Jamie's mum had always struck me as a very sharp lady. She often used to study me in a strange way, almost as if she knew what was going through my mind. And she was always asking me when I last ate, as if to imply I was neglected at home, which, of course, to a certain degree, I was.

We sat like a couple of right plonkers in the Beetle in Jamie's lock-up, panicking because we were already running late for those girls in Guildford. I rolled down the window and got out and started pushing the Beetle backwards out of that garage. It weighed a bloody ton compared with Kevin's mum's Mini Cooper, which was the last vehicle I'd had to push, when Kevin and I rolled it into his family garage to avoid anyone hearing us using the car.

So here we were: two highly irresponsible teenagers pushing a bright-orange VW Beetle out into a street in respectable middle-class suburbia, so we could bump-start it and risk life and limb to meet a couple of girls twenty-five miles away who thought we were at least three years older than we really were.

Controlling the VW was tricky even as we pushed it onto the street before attempting the bump-start. The steering was like treacle, the exact opposite of the Triumph or the Jag Mark II, which had both had power steering. It was difficult even to control it as I tried to line it up on the road. The other problem was that the street outside Jamie's house was as flat as the proverbial pancake. There was no dip in the road with which to try to pick up some decent speed for a successful bump-start.

Ten minutes later and we must have pushed the Beetle at least a quarter of a mile without any success. We just couldn't get up enough speed to get the engine to turn over. We were about to push the Beetle all the way back to his house when I spotted a dip in the road about one hundred yards ahead and managed to persuade Jamie to give it one more try. I was instantly re-energised because I was convinced we'd now actually start the Beetle.

We finally got the car to the brow of the hill, and I explained to Jamie that once I'd jumped into the Beetle as it started rolling down the hill, I'd let it pick up lots of speed before letting the clutch off. That meant he'd have to meet me at the bottom of the hill. He looked a bit worried, but I don't think he had the energy to argue with me.

CAR TROUBLE

We both gave it a slight push and then I jumped in, rammed the gear stick into second and waited for it to pick up speed. I let out the clutch when the speedometer said 15 mph. Nothing. Just a lot of shuddering. I slammed my foot down on the clutch and let it pick up more speed. Exactly the same happened again. I did it a third time before running out of hill and managing to just brake to a halt a few feet from an incredibly busy crossing, where traffic was flowing at high speed. I was just thankful it stopped where it did, and I sat in the car, completely stumped.

I'd run out of ideas, and it was only when other cars began hooting at me to move that I banged on the emergency indicators and waited for Jamie to get down the hill. The thought of pushing the car all the way up the hill and back to his house was daunting.

Suddenly, a big gold signet ring tapped on the window, snapping me out of my mini-meltdown. It belonged to a jet-black hand. I looked up, and a West Indian in a London Transport uniform, with a ticket machine hanging round his neck, was smiling at me. His teeth seemed luminous in the darkness.

'You gotta move dis, man. We can't get by.'

I turned around and a red double-decker Routemaster was sitting right on my tail, its diesel engine throbbing. I apologised profusely and immediately jumped out and started trying, with no success, to push the Beetle. I'd run out of energy, and it wasn't moving.

'Open de boot, man,' said the bus conductor. I could smell the familiar musty whiff of cannabis resin coming from his direction.

'What?'

'Open it up, man. Maybe we can fix it.'

But he'd just said the 'boot', hadn't he? It was only then I remembered the engine was in the boot of the Beetle.

The bus driver hooted impatiently, but my new mate, his conductor, just waved him away and shouted, 'Wait up, man.'

Meanwhile I leaned under the steering wheel and tried to find the boot lever. Nothing. I scrambled around desperately, but there was no sign of anything. Behind me, the bus conductor was fiddling about also trying to work out how to open the boot.

'Bingo!' he shouted. I looked in my rear-view as the boot lid flipped up. Thank God he'd found it. Maybe he could get the car started. I jumped back out of the driver's door and caught the eye of the bus driver, who looked very pissed off, sucking on a huge pipe and tapping his fingers on the Routemaster's huge steering wheel.

'We're gonna get a right bollocking when we get to Willesden,' he yelled at his colleague. But his conductor was buried in the boot.

As I moved alongside him, he gave out a yell, wheezed heavily and started laughing uncontrollably. I didn't know what the hell was going on. Then he popped his head up from the boot, clutching a piece of paper.

'Your name Jamie?' he asked.

I couldn't be bothered to complicate matters further by saying 'no', so I nodded.

He held up the note and gave it to me.

It read:

Jamie. I've taken the distributor cap out just in case you decided to borrow my car. Love Mum.

The funny thing was that I wasn't in the least bit surprised. Jamie's mum had us both sussed.

The bus conductor kindly helped me push the Beetle to the side of the road and then headed off on his Routemaster. He waved and laughed from the platform as it passed, and I smiled back. We'd been well and truly snookered. In Guildford, those two girls gave up waiting for us and went home, never to be seen again.

We scraped together enough money to get the car towed back to Jamie's house by a local garage. I lost that note so Jamie's mum must have known we'd tried to 'borrow' her Beetle when she got back from her holiday. But she never said a word when I next saw her.

Maybe my weird life as a child driver was not so secret after all?

THIS IS THE THIRD PART!

Setting off for a spin in the Triumph 2000.

GREAT RIDE, SHAME ABOUT THE LAMP POST

FOLLOWING THE DISAPPOINTMENT OF MY DISASTROUS FIRST ever blind date and that attempt to nick Jamie's mum's Beetle, my mother started making it much harder for me to find her spare set of car keys. I guess she must have sussed out what I was up to, although she never once confronted me about stealing the Triumph. Maybe she felt a bit guilty because she was the one who'd got me into 'real' driving in the first place. Anyway, whatever the truth of the matter, my 'supply' had just been cut off at the main source and I needed to start looking elsewhere for opportunities to improve my driving skills.

Not long after that, I was out with some of my new, slightly older friends, one of whom lived in posh St George's Hills, Weybridge, where John Lennon and Cliff Richard resided. St George's Hills was a sprawling series of hills on which were built some of the biggest detached houses I had ever seen in my life. My friend's parents lived in one of the area's smaller residences, and we'd trooped back to his place to have a look at an old Ford Popular that had been in his garage for years. My friend reckoned it only needed a bit of work on it to get it going again. We had a close look at it, but it was a non-starter in every sense of the word, so we all felt a bit deflated because we'd hoped to get the Popular started and do a bit of reckless joyriding over that weekend.

Eventually, my mate's mother got so fed up of having us hanging around the house that she literally pushed us out of the front door and told us to walk down to Weybridge town centre to get out of her hair. We set off in a bit of huff and stomped along the main road near his house, heads down, thoroughly irritated. Four typical moody youths.

That's when I spotted a brand-new Jaguar XJ6 parked up on the side of the road. It caught my eye because the XJ6 had only just come out and it had been anointed by the press as a successor to the beloved Mark II, which my mother and I had enjoyed driving so much. This particular XJ6 was in classic maroon and it looked pretty impressive, with its low-slung undercarriage and a menacing-looking chrome grille staring up at me and my friends as we approached. The XJ6 was a much bigger, scarier 'cat' than the Mark II.

The street was deserted, and it was obvious from the angle of the XJ6 that the owner had slung it up on the kerb in a bit of a hurry. We were still walking towards it at this stage and I was in no hurry because I was examining it in minute detail. I wanted to take a look at the speedometer to see what the last speed was on the dial. I had a little bet with myself that it would be '160'. I loved it when car speedometers went up to such high figures, even though most of them were never actually capable of going that fast. As we strolled slowly past the XJ6, I peered in through the window for a closer look at the speedo. Hmmmmm. It said '160'! That was ridiculous. Mind you, my mum had once got the old Mark II up to about 134 mph and the last number on that speedo had been 140.

That's when I noticed the keys in the ignition. I did a double take back to the speedometer before returning to the key and it was definitely in there. The owner had left the key to his brand-new XJ6 in the ignition. 'He must be a bloody idiot,' was my first thought. My second thought kicked in very quickly after that.

I want to steal that car.

I didn't say it out loud. I just let us all carry on past the XJ6 for

GREAT RIDE, SHAME ABOUT THE LAMP POST

about 50 yards. None of my mates had spotted the key. Then I stopped them in a huddle.

'The key's in that car,' I said. At first my friends Billy, Robert and Steve said nothing, so I repeated myself. 'The key's in the bloody car. Let's nick it.'

Billy took a big gulp and then nodded his head. 'Yeah. Let's do it.'

The other two, Robert and Steve, looked a bit less certain. Then Robert blurted out, 'But we don't know how to drive it.'

Billy smiled right at me. 'Yeah, but you do, don't you?'

Billy had been one of the few people I'd confessed my driving skills to. And he was right. The XJ6 couldn't be that different from the old Mark II. The dashboard had looked pretty similar when we walked past it. I looked back at the XJ6 and scanned around for anyone else on the street. It was still dead quiet.

'You two wait here,' I said to Robert and Steve.

Billy and I virtually ran back to the XJ6, continually looking around in case the owner reappeared. I'd worked out he must be in the house next to where he'd parked the car. And there was no one looking out of any of the windows.

We'd just got back to the car when I heard a vehicle coming from the opposite direction at high speed. It was a police panda car, and it must have been doing at least 50. 'Shit! They're already onto us,' I thought. My two other mates had dived into the bushes the moment they saw the police.

The car's blue light was flashing as it raced past without even giving us a second glance. Obviously there were bigger crimes to solve in St George's Hills that day. I watched as the panda swept around a corner and out of sight. This was still too big an opportunity to turn down. I wanted to drive that car.

'Let's do it,' I said to Billy. He didn't seem worried so I grabbed the handle and opened the driver's door. He swept round to the passenger side. We were both looking in all directions, just in case we were spotted.

Luckily the XJ6 had a very similar starter system to the Mark II, so I flicked the key on and pressed hard with my thumb and the 2.8

engine roared into life. Well, it sounded like a roar to me at the time, but it was probably quite quiet. Billy looked terrified. His eyes were flaring and he obviously was lost for words.

I smiled over at him and let out the handbrake and pushed the column gear change into 'D' for Drive. We moved off very gently because it had a smaller engine than my mother's 3.4 Mark II and it was a much heavier motor car. The two other boys were dusting themselves down after diving into that hedge earlier as I rolled up alongside them.

'You coming or what?' I said as the electric window glided downwards. It was the first time I had ever used an electric window. I felt like a king.

Robert and Steve looked at each other and then just shrugged their shoulders before jumping into the back of the car. I waited for a moment after hearing sirens in the distance.

At the crossroads ahead, two more police panda cars raced across us. We were the last thing on their minds. It made me feel strangely reassured that they were all so busy on other things.

The XJ6 was very different from the Mark II to handle so I drove quite gingerly up the road at first. It seemed to jerk quite badly because the accelerator seemed over-sensitive to my touch. After about another hundred yards I started to get a proper feel for the car, and my three mates were laughing nervously because they couldn't quite believe that we'd actually stolen a car in the middle of St George's Hills. I kept checking my rear-view, just in case someone was chasing us, but there was no sign of life from the house next to where we had taken the Jag from.

It was while I was checking out the rear-view that a dog came bounding into the road right in front of us. I only noticed it when Billy shouted out, 'Watch it! There's a dog.' I looked down from the rear-view, spotted it just in time and swerved to avoid it. Suddenly everything went into slow motion as we slewed straight into a lamp post. We were thrown forward, but not seriously because of the slow speed we were travelling at. But I was shocked at how much damage that lamp post had caused. When I tried to get out the driver's door, it wouldn't budge.

GREAT RIDE, SHAME ABOUT THE LAMP POST

Eventually we scrambled out of the back doors, which did open, and I was stunned to find that the lamp post had driven itself right through the middle of the bonnet in the crash. Steve and Robert were both long gone by the time Billy and I paused for breath, about ten yards from the pranged Jag. We looked around in all directions, but there was no sign of anyone, which was a relief.

Two more police cars rattled past the crossroads a few hundred yards ahead of us, and it was dawning on me that something very serious was happening in this neck of the woods. Then I saw a police van pull up on the next corner and about half a dozen uniformed bobbies clambered out and started walking off in all directions. I wasn't sure if they'd spotted us or not. It didn't make sense that they would know about us so quickly. They couldn't be searching for us, surely? But I couldn't take that chance so I told Billy we needed to split up. I was more infuriated with myself for being such a crap driver.

I nodded at Billy as he wandered off in the opposite direction and then dived up a side road. Eventually I found a row of hedges to hide under. I crouched down on the grass behind the hedge. I was so nervous I could hear my own breathing. I just hoped no one else could. I waited there for at least five minutes, wondering what had happened to my friends. The last I'd seen of Billy was when he'd started scrambling down an embankment as I turned up this street.

My breath had only just slowed down to a normal level when I heard voices while I was hidden under that hedgerow. I held my breath. Two pairs of huge black boots stomped past me, just a couple of feet away.

'D'you really think a bunch of kids did it?' one policeman said to the other.

'Kids these days, son. They're out of control,' replied his mate.

It suddenly dawned on me that perhaps the police were connecting what had alerted all those police cars with the theft of the XJ6. That was bad news all round. I continued holding my breath until I was sure they weren't coming back. I was even more nervous now. We all needed to get off St George's Hills without being arrested, but it was going to be bloody tricky.

CAR TROUBLE

I lay there under the hedgerow for another half an hour, waiting to see if there was any more police activity, before deciding that I had to try to make a run for it, otherwise it would be dark soon and I'd never manage to get away. I knew I needed to walk to Weybridge railway station in order to get home and it was about a mile away.

It was almost dusk by the time I scrambled to my feet. I kept myself carefully hidden behind the hedgerow while I brushed myself down. It seemed deserted out on the road so I moved swiftly and quietly along the pavement, careful not to let any passing headlights illuminate me. I'd just turned the corner into the main road down to Weybridge station and was keeping to the grass verge when a hand grabbed me from behind by the collar. 'Where d'you think you're going, then?'

I was pushed to the ground and my right arm was pulled up behind my back. A knee was pressing hard against the small of my back.

'You're nicked, son.'

I didn't respond at first because I didn't want to incriminate myself until I knew why there were so many coppers in the area in the first place.

'What's going on? I'm just on my way home from my friend's house.'

'And where's that?'

I was about to supply Robert's home address when I realised that might incriminate myself even further if they'd already arrested him. I wasn't sure of how to answer so I said nothing more. I knew that 3 p.m. was about the time we'd stolen the Jag and I didn't want to let them nick me for that. They stood there and repeatedly asked me about my friend's address, but I still refused to respond.

One of them got on the walkie-talkie while the other held onto me. Minutes later, I was being bundled into the back of a Ford Escort panda car. I hadn't got a clue what was going on.

We didn't go far. It couldn't have been more than a quarter of a mile. The panda slowed down as it approached three or four bungalows, which were very modest compared with many of the massive properties on St George's Hills. That's when I noticed at least ten police vehicles and dozens of officers going in and out of one of the bungalows.

GREAT RIDE, SHAME ABOUT THE LAMP POST

Then the panda turned a corner and we came onto the same road where we'd nicked the Jag earlier. Eventually the panda slowed down just near the smashed up XJ6, which hadn't budged since I'd driven it into that lamp post earlier.

I was manhandled out of the back seat of the two-door Ford Escort. Two cops then hauled me up in front of a rather frail-looking old lady, who was standing at what I presumed was the end of the pathway to her house.

'Is this one of them?' one of the coppers asked her.

I looked away in the opposite direction from the mangled-up Jag and waited to be arrested. I presumed she must have seen us from her front window as we piled out of the Jag. It was a clear view.

'I'm not sure,' she mumbled, examining me very closely through thick Coke-bottle lenses.

'What?' said the more irritating of the two policemen.

The old lady looked quite upset by now because she obviously felt the police were putting pressure on her.

'I told you I'm not sure.'

'Well, madam. You need to be positive if you think this is one of the lads' – he nodded in the direction of the Jag – 'you saw getting out of that car.'

The old lady took another deep, noisy breath.

'No. No. It's not one of them. You can let this poor boy go. I should think his parents are worried half to death about him.'

'If only,' I thought to myself.

The older copper was a right comedian. 'It's your lucky day, son. On yer bike. Go on. Scram.'

I ran as fast as I could down the hill and through the woods to Weybridge station. I never wanted to go to St George's Hills ever again.

It was only the next day when I picked up the *Daily Mirror*, which I always read without fail before breakfast, that I discovered an old lady from one of the bungalows I'd passed in the panda car had been murdered and the police were convinced the killers had stolen the XJ6 and then smashed it up on that lamp post.

GOING IN CIRCLES IN A ROVER 3-LITRE COUPE

THE INCIDENT WITH THE XJ6 WAS A BIT OF A WAKE-UP CALL for me because it made me feel that it would be a lot safer if I just bought myself an old banger, rather than being tempted by any more taking-and-driving-away opportunities.

My 14th birthday was fast approaching and I'd managed to save up £120 from the sale of Tuinal capsules to my friends over the previous few months. So one day I picked up the *Evening Standard* and looked up the classified section for used cars.

I didn't really give much thought to exactly what model I wanted. I had so little money it just needed to be a 'decent runner', which was one of the most popular phrases in the second-hand car business back then. I was hoping for a meaty car with a pokey engine for about a hundred quid. I didn't worry about insurance or tax or MOTs. I settled on an advert for a Rover 3-Litre Coupe. I have no idea why they were called coupes because they were huge tanks with four doors and couldn't have looked less sporty if they'd tried, although they did have a distinct slope at the back, so I guess that's where the coupe bit came in.

My first mistake was taking the cash along with me when I went to view the car in a scrapyard in North Kensington. The guy who was selling it didn't even seem to know how many miles it had on the clock, and the yard was full of marauding Alsatians who kept barking at us and sticking their noses between my legs, which didn't exactly help my concentration.

I never once questioned why the car itself was up for sale in a yard full of mashed-up accident-damaged vehicles. But I didn't have any experience of buying cars so I just plonked down the cash and drove the Rover home. That was my first mistake. It was a terrifying car to drive and handled like a Chieftain tank. By the time I got to Ladbroke Grove I was losing confidence fast and also convinced that someone would mug me at every set of traffic lights.

Back in those days, Notting Hill wasn't full of the landed gentry of today. It was buzzing with dodgy-looking characters on street corners, and when I was younger my parents studiously avoided driving there. It was looked on as a virtual ghetto full of people 'who'd only just got off the boat', as my dad used to say.

Anyway. I then attempted, with some difficulty, to negotiate my way through the narrow streets of Holland Park en route back to my parents' house, but I was still struggling to handle the sheer bulk of the Rover, which was best known at the time for ferrying around senior politicians.

After narrowly avoiding killing two pedestrians at the end of my road when I drove through a red light, I knew that the Rover Coupe was in serious danger of regressing my driving skills. My parents were away at the time so I rather recklessly squeezed it into the carport in front of our house and got straight on the phone to the previous owner to ask him if he wanted to buy it back. He was knocking on my front door inside an hour and ended up paying me half what I'd just paid for it, but I didn't care. I just wanted to get rid of the monster before it devoured me.

NON-STOP TO PLYMOUTH IN A CORTINA

MY PARENTS MIGHT HAVE BEEN IRRESPONSIBLE, SELFISH AND insular, but they were incredibly generous when it came to trust. By the time I reached 14, my mother had decided she should tell my father about my driving skills and was determined to convince him I could be relied upon to drive them short distances around London.

I was delighted to be their chauffeur. I didn't care how drunk they got. In fact, the more pissed the better because I could then put my foot on the gas and they'd be too inebriated to care. In other words, they gave me a free rein to drive how I pleased. And we even agreed that if I got stopped my mother would insist to police that she was teaching me how to drive and my L-plates must have fallen off. I shared exactly the same name with my father, so I could pretend to be him if the police insisted on driving licences being produced.

So now we were all in it up to our necks, but at least we were in it together. For all their failings, my parents' complete and utter recklessness had its advantages. Driving my parents around was also significant in other ways. I was once again parenting my parents; driving them around and waiting for them outside pubs and bars was a bit like being the typical dad waiting patiently outside the disco in his slippers. No wonder I couldn't wait to leave school and join the real world where people drove *all* the time.

Often I'd drop my parents off somewhere and then take the Triumph for a spin before returning to pick them up. I longed for them to let me take them somewhere in the country because I wanted to put my foot down and do a proper road trip, rather than sitting in clogged-up traffic in the West End.

Then along came my first proper long-distance drive under the most bizarre circumstances, even by the weird standards of my dysfunctional upbringing. My parents were still great party-givers, and by this time I was also allowed to act as unofficial valet for their guests' cars when they showed up at our house for functions.

That meant opening the car doors when they arrived and offering to park their vehicles nearby. No one seemed to even attempt to question my age by this time. In fact, I don't think most of my parents' drunken mates knew how old I was, and if they did, they certainly didn't seem to care. As I mentioned earlier, I looked about 17 by now in any case. And my parents never once admitted my true age to any of the guests when I was 'working' as the in-house valet.

One couple were so impressed with my careful driving skills when I parked up their Ford Cortina that they offered me twenty quid to drive them home later that evening. Twenty quid was a small fortune to me back in those days. But then the man added very quickly: 'Trains back to London from Plymouth run every hour.'

Plymouth? I didn't even know where Plymouth was exactly, but I wasn't about to throw away my first ever professional driving job, so I nodded my head and did my best not to look too surprised in case they started wondering if I was the right man for the job.

My mother only got wind of my long-distance driving job when the man mentioned it in passing to her. I saw her hesitate for a split second but then assure the man what a good driver I was.

Within an hour I was driving up the M4, aged 14, at the start of a marathon journey across England. The couple were half-cut and seemed perfectly happy sitting together in the back seat. It suited me because the last thing I wanted to do was make polite conversation.

NON-STOP TO PLYMOUTH IN A CORTINA

Never once did they even ask if I had a full licence. I don't think it ever crossed their minds. As usual I put all those tips from my dad's chauffeur to good use. I loved it when the woman commented on what a good driver I was. I watched the road avidly and tried my hardest to make sure the journey wasn't too wobbly or uncomfortable.

As a reward, they gave me a fiver tip when we got to Plymouth and obviously covered my train journey back to London. Once again, I learned how nice it was to be appreciated, especially when it came to driving. It also further fuelled my obsession with getting a job. School was a waste of time for me. I wanted to get out there into the real world and drive a car and enjoy the freedom that came with that sort of independence.

HITTING THE HOME STRAIGHT

MY MOTHER KNEW THAT SO LONG AS SHE ENCOURAGED MY driving I'd continue to have a very strong sense of loyalty towards her. She was far from perfect, but if anyone tried to suggest anything was wrong with her, then they'd have to answer to me.

One day my mother showed up at my senior school in the white Triumph 2000 to watch me playing rugby on the playing fields next to the main building. She was decked out in a cringe-making multicoloured knitted party dress beneath a fur coat. It was only October so it was hardly cold. Naturally, all the other parents were in wellies and Barbour jackets, which made it even more embarrassing for me.

From the moment she arrived I lost all my concentration and started being bollocked almost non-stop by the school coach, who couldn't understand why I was suddenly playing so badly. We were trounced 48–0, and as I trooped off at the end, my mother tottered across the mud in her heels and demanded a kiss on both cheeks. I felt duty-bound to oblige, even though I could feel all my schoolmates watching. But I did my 'duty' and then headed off towards the changing rooms.

As I walked in, a boy by the name of David Golden was leaning up against my locker, sneering right at me. I knew immediately what was on his mind. He was always trying to humiliate other kids. I looked down in the hope he'd not say anything. I should have known better. 'Why did you kiss your mother? She looks really weird.'

I looked up and tilted my head for a moment. Golden wouldn't leave it alone.

'Nancy boy. Nancy boy. Clarkson kissed his mummy.'

My eyes misted over. I tried to push him aside to open my locker.

'Clarkson kissed his mummy. Clarkson kissed his mummy.'

Those words were ringing in my head over and over by this time.

'Clarkson kissed his mummy. Clarkson kissed his mummy.'

I punched Golden squarely in the nose and felt it crack before blood began spurting down from his right nostril. Then I moved in closer and threw my fists into his chest before catching him with an uppercut under his chin, which threw his head back.

'Clarkson kissed his mummy. Clarkson kissed his mummy.'

Golden's words continued ringing in my head over and over again, fuelling my anger, so I kept steaming into him. Everything became a blur. When he fell to the floor I began kicking out at him with my football boots. I was about to rake my studs across his face when two teachers just managed to drag me off him. I didn't resist them because I had done what I set out to do and there was no need to involve anyone else.

I was marched straight off to the headmaster's office and was expelled on the spot. They'd been waiting for an excuse for years. My mother drove me home without saying a word in the Triumph, and once again I drifted into my own little motoring netherworld, while studiously watching her driving. I think Procol Harum's 'A Whiter Shade of Pale' was playing, which we both liked. I wasn't bothered about being kicked out of school. I'd been ready to head off into the so-called real world since I was about 12. I turned towards my mother, next to me, and said, 'Can I drive?' My mother tried her hardest not to smile, but I caught a glimpse of those gappy front teeth and I knew she was laughing inside. Ten minutes later she pulled over and let me have a quick spin.

And I still don't know to this day if my father even knew I had been expelled.

THE TOPLESS VITESSE CONVERTIBLE

MY MATE BILLY – THE GUY WHO'D BEEN WITH ME WHEN WE stole that XJ6 in St George's Hills – and I were always coming up with money-making schemes. He was the guy who'd suggested flogging my mum's Tuinal tranquillisers.

Billy's family lived in a house on a hill near the All England Tennis Club, where the world-famous Wimbledon tournament was held every year. His parents were both teachers and they often travelled abroad on trips with the school where they both worked. The 1971 Championships, in the last week of June and first week of July, marked yet another benchmark when it came to developing my driving skills. The fact John Newcombe won the men's trophy and Evonne Goolagong Cawley the women's that year didn't mean much to either of us. We had other priorities.

Billy and I were lazing around listening to Neil Young and puffing on a bit of substandard Lebanese Black when we came up with an idea that could potentially make us a small fortune over the following fortnight. Billy's parents were abroad at the time, and I'd noticed earlier on the walk down to his house that some of his neighbours were turning their front gardens into bargain parking spaces for the thousands of visitors to Wimbledon.

Now here I was sucking on a joint looking out of the front window of Billy's house at a completely open lawn on which you could park at least five cars at a rate of one pound a day per vehicle. That would mean five quid a day over twelve days, which came to a very healthy sixty quid. Not to be sniffed at.

So we mocked up some cardboard signs with slightly stoned swirly writing, which said, 'Cheap Parking: One Pound a Day'. I took one sign up to the corner of the road, so people passing by would spot our 'services'. Billy put another huge sign up right outside the house and we went back inside to toke on some more joints, listen to happy-go-lucky Leonard Cohen and have the occasional laugh at the TV news, which featured a rather awful plane crash on that evening's bulletin.

I don't know what time we fell asleep, but neither of us made it to a bed and we conked out on a couple of sofas. Suddenly a loud hooting sound cut right through my head. It felt like a car was in the sitting room next to me. I struggled to open my eyes. Then another hooting noise virtually shook the room. I struggled to get up and looked out the front window, where there was a massive Humber Sceptre sitting with its huge, nasty-looking grille staring straight at me. Our first 'customer' had arrived. We'd overslept and it was already midday.

I bounded outside and took one day's parking fee off a big middle-aged man with a fedora and a long cigar who looked like a 1950s gangster. I was about to go back into the house when he called after me, 'Hang about. You need these, don't you?'

As I turned to face him, he threw me the keys to the Humber. I only just caught them. Neither Billy nor I had even considered they might entrust us with the keys to their cars. I clasped the keys tight in the palm of my hand and tried hard to push my mind away from all the possible driving scenarios connected to that Humber.

But it didn't work. That guy would be out all day until at least five or six. That was at least a couple of hours of driving time. No. No. No. I tried to push the keys into my pocket as if that would somehow stop me being tempted.

THE TOPLESS VITESSE CONVERTIBLE

Billy stumbled out of the front door, having finally woken up to the fact that we'd just had our first customer. I decided not to tell him I had the keys in case he tried to dissuade me from borrowing the Sceptre. I needed a few minutes to compose myself and think through the consequences of my actions *if* I decided to go for a ride.

Obviously those keys were still burning a big hole in my pocket. I went inside with Billy and we had a wash and brush up and a bowl of cornflakes in preparation for some more customers. Sitting at his kitchen table I couldn't hold back any more, so I slapped the keys to the Humber down in front of me.

A huge Cheshire-cat grin came over Billy's face when he clapped eyes on the keys. But we both sat there and said nothing.

'We can't do it,' I said in the most matter-of-fact voice I could muster.

'Why not?' came his reply.

'We'll end up in prison.'

'He'll never know.'

'Hang on. Last time I got in a car with you I ended up wrapping it around a lamp post.'

Our conversation was interrupted by another loud car hooter. It seemed that our swirly potted-out pseudo-psychedelic signs were attracting more customers than any of Billy's more straight-laced neighbours. Outside were two women in a Triumph Herald. This time both of us went out to greet them. They took one look at us and drove off. Oh well. Their loss.

But that interruption did us one big favour because it made me realise that we should wait until we had all five spaces occupied before I went back to the subject of joyriding. It didn't take long for four more cars to park up and *all* of them volunteered their keys. I was surprised that these motorists were so trusting, but then Billy reminded me we were in an upmarket area and we both looked like (and indeed had been) a couple of public schoolboys.

So we retreated back to the kitchen to discuss our next move.

'I rather like the look of the Rover 2000,' said Billy.

'I prefer the Granada,' I said.

'Nah. That Vitesse is a cracker.'

'This is mad. What about a compromise and let's just take the Humber.'

'Nah. That gangster looked like he'd shoot us if he found out.'

And so it went on and on with absolutely no decision being forthcoming. Time was passing, and if we didn't make up our minds soon we wouldn't have time to take any of the cars anywhere.

I took one of my classic long, deep breaths, then announced: 'Fuck it. Let's give the Vitesse a spin.' It was the easiest one to drive in and out because it had been the last one parked up on Billy's front lawn.

Five minutes later we were sitting in a traffic jam at the end of Billy's road, having only managed to half flip up the canvas convertible roof. What we also hadn't bargained for was the endless streams of traffic near the All England Club. So much for a joyride. We must have sat in that traffic jam for at least half an hour.

The Vitesse had the potential to be a very pokey motor thanks to a meaty two-litre engine and a very neat little gear shift stick. Finally we got some speed up on the edge of Wimbledon Common and sat back and enjoyed the ride.

Then I looked down at the clock on the dash and saw that it was 3.30 p.m. We'd been very careful earlier to ask each customer what time they reckoned they'd be back, and I suddenly remembered that the couple with the Vitesse had said four o'clock.

'Shit. We'd better turn around,' I yelled, with the wind whistling around our ears. Billy gave me one of those worried looks like he'd flashed at me after I pranged that XJ6 in St George's Hills.

I took a left off the Common and started winding my way back down to Billy's road. That's when we hit yet more traffic log-jams. We sat not moving for ten minutes in a queue of cars and nervously counted down the time on the Vitesse's dashboard clock.

That's when I looked up and spotted a familiar-looking couple wandering just ahead of us. Shit. It was the pair who owned the Vitesse. I had no choice but to do a quick three-point turn before they turned round and spotted us. But that meant we were now even further away from Billy's house. I hung a right back onto the road alongside Wimbledon Common and tried to nip down another road that might eventually lead to Billy's street, but that was also thick with traffic.

I told Billy that if we got caught we'd say we were just taking the car round the corner to make way for another one of our customers who was jammed in.

'Great idea, except for one thing. What if none of the other cars have been moved?' said Billy, slowly pulling out all the other pairs of car keys, which happened to be in his pocket.

'Why have you got them all on you?' I asked in a much more panicky tone.

'Cos there's no one else to move them, is there? Dummy.'

We were deep in shit now: sitting in a traffic jam half a mile from Billy's house, knowing that the owners of the car we were driving would be arriving back at his place at any minute and wondering where the hell their car was. They'd be sure to call the police.

A few long beats of silent fear followed.

Then something happened that really wasn't all that surprising for Wimbledon fortnight.

It began raining.

'Shit. Shit. Shit.' For once in our lives, Billy and I said something completely in unison with each other.

We both started trying to pull the canvas roof back over us, but it wouldn't budge. I looked at the clock just to make myself feel even worse. It was 4.05 p.m. They were probably already there and in the next couple of minutes Wimbledon police would be alerted to the theft of their Vitesse and the chief suspects would be the two kids who'd rented them some parking space.

Meanwhile I was in danger of ripping the canvas roof off its hinges because it refused to budge and the rain was coming down hard. Billy jumped out of the car and tried to help, but then the traffic started moving ahead of us and everyone began hooting, so we got back into the Vitesse with the canvas roof still half up. It was a complete disaster. I was almost tempted to divert the car to Wimbledon Police Station and surrender in the hope we'd get a lighter sentence.

The traffic finally cleared and within a couple of minutes we were turning into Billy's street. At least there were no flashing blue lights outside his house, about two hundred yards ahead. But we still had the problem of the canvas roof, which was sticking up in the air. Billy took another tug at it, and by some miracle it worked this time. Billy leaned across and snapped the bolts on each corner of the windscreen and then started trying to dry the wet dashboard with the sleeve of his shirt. I looked ahead, fully expecting the owners to be waiting outside Billy's house in a fury, but they were nowhere to be seen. Maybe they'd gone down to the police station?

Anyway, I drove the Vitesse straight back into its original parking place and we both sat there, waiting for the handcuffs to appear at any second. When it finally dawned on me that we were not in trouble after all, I slung Billy a cloth from the chair by the front door and told him to make out he was giving it a friendly polish. All part of the service, eh?

A few minutes later, the couple who owned the Vitesse appeared from the other direction. God knows how they'd managed to take 20 minutes to walk a few hundred yards, but I wasn't complaining. And they were so impressed that we were giving the car a quick polish, they bunged us a ten-bob tip.

As I waved the Vitesse off, I wondered how the hell we'd got away with that one. In some ways I wished I'd been caught because now I was looking at the other four cars on Billy's front lawn and wondering if we had time to take another one for a quick joyride. A few minutes later I settled back at the kitchen table, but Billy quickly read my mind. 'Don't even go there. We are *not* taking another car. End of story.'

He was right, of course, but, hey, there was always tomorrow.

MISS HOGG AND A BEDFORD 7-TONNER

TOWARDS THE END OF 1970, MY PARENTS GRADUALLY BEGAN moving out of the London house to spend more time at their newly acquired cottage close to the sea, near Brighton. I was delighted to be going back to an empty home virtually every night. In a sense I was relieved because I didn't have to worry about them so much if they weren't there. They had their own life and I had mine. I didn't feel as if I had been 'abandoned'.

But the one problem with living at home on my own was that the steady supply of my mother's Tuinal was drying up and I needed to earn some cash in order to have a life outside the house and keep up with my mates, most of whom had also left school. I got two friends to pay rent for a bedroom they shared in the basement, but most of that had to go to my mother.

Then I managed to get a part-time job as a lorry driver's mate for Coca-Cola after answering an advert in a job centre. Back then it was possible to get part-time jobs at 14 and over. It was the perfect job for me because I got to go out all day in a massive Bedford 7-ton truck. I usually worked with a driver called Brendan, who had a huge handlebar moustache and lived in Bromley, a place I had never been to or even heard of in my short life.

I got on well with Brendan. But he had no idea about my middle-class background because I'd immediately played down my 'posh' accent so I could mix in more easily with all the Coca-Cola people. I knew they'd never accept me if I sounded as if I had a plum in my mouth.

The 'manor' I covered for Coca-Cola was West London, so I became Brendan's navigator because I knew the area so well. He quickly trusted me, and I diverted his attention away from my roots by showing an interest in his home life with his young wife and a baby. I was quite envious, in a sense, because he seemed to have a support system around him.

Brendan showed great patience and understanding while I was 'bedding in', even when I dropped a whole crate of Coke bottles during one pick-up. That cost us a lot of cash because they were all returnable bottles. Brendan also taught me how we could top up our salaries by keeping up to ten crates of empties from various customers and then creating a new client from whom we 'picked them up' so we could pocket the cash for those empties.

I much preferred working for Coca-Cola than going to school, and at weekends I mixed with my latest group of friends, who were mainly from working-class backgrounds. I liked the way that people accepted me more if they didn't think I was 'posh'.

Back on the Coca-Cola lorries I was having a ball. I liked the way we jumped down from the high cab and then clambered back into it after a delivery. I also noticed that other, smaller vehicles literally looked up to us in our massive lorry.

I studied Brendan's driving skills very closely, and occasionally, when there were two pubs a hundred yards apart, he'd allow me to go behind the wheel and drive the lorry, but only up to second gear. The first time I did it I underestimated the sensitivity of the air-brakes and slammed too hard on the pedal, and we both heard all the crates of Coca-Cola crashing forward. Brendan just laughed and luckily only a few bottles got smashed. I soon learned how to gently stroke those air-brakes, so it didn't happen again.

I also quickly picked up on the rougher edges of Brendan's attitude and opinions. We'd both admire the same girls in the street and laugh and talk about a lot of the same stuff we'd both watched on the previous night's telly.

I never once pushed Brendan to let me go behind the wheel because I knew he'd be in serious trouble if anyone back at the depot found out. He always volunteered to let me drive and he remained very careful not to let me take it more than about a hundred yards at a time. But he said I was a good driver right from the beginning. I loved the sound of the diesel engine revving up before taking off in first gear. It was a much more gradual build-up than with a car, but once it took off the feeling of power behind the wheel was immense, especially for a 14-year-old kid.

We usually set off from the Coca-Cola depot at about 7 a.m., but I was never once late, even though it was a nightmare bus journey for me. I'd always been an early riser thanks to all that traffic in our street.

One morning Brendan was uncharacteristically running late. We were supposed to set off at seven on the dot, as we had many more drop-offs than usual because one of the other drivers was off sick and we were covering for him as well as doing our usual 'rounds'. Brendan eventually turned up just before 8 a.m. He looked red in the face and said he had the flu. It wasn't until we'd left the depot that he revealed he was hungover after his wife had thrown him out of the house when they'd had a row. He was in no fit state to work, and I soon noticed his driving was atrocious. He kept almost clipping cars by cutting corners and he had to concentrate so carefully that he hardly uttered a word for the next couple of hours. We struggled from pub to pub, delivering crates of Coca-Cola and picking up empties as we went along. At one stage, Brendan even went off to vomit round the back of the lorry after we'd barrowed about forty crates of Coca-Cola down some very tricky basement stairs. He was all over the place. I tried to take the strain off him by doing a lot of the humping, but I knew we'd never get all our rounds completed in time if he didn't pull his weight more. Brendan didn't expand much more on his domestic problems, either.

We eventually arrived at a pub at the Kensington High Street end of the busy Earls Court Road, which was very near where I lived. And the pub itself was on the same corner where aged five I'd once nearly been run over by a Bristol on my way to school. This particular pub was a very awkward place to deliver to. We had to sling the Bedford up tight on the pavement, and then one of us would go down to the cellar and open the trapdoors so we could sling the crates down one at a time. I was usually the one up by the lorry, but Brendan was feeling so hungover by this stage that he insisted on me going down to the cellar.

It was damp and dark down there, and when the trapdoors opened up and I looked up at Brendan it didn't exactly fill me with confidence. He was swaying so much on his feet he almost fell in. Moments later he began dropping the crates down to me at an alarming angle. I only just managed to hang onto them.

Inevitably I ended up dropping a couple of crates in that cellar and all the bottles smashed everywhere. Initially Brendan seemed really pissed off with me, and I felt guilty for letting him down, even though it wasn't really my fault. I eventually navigated my way through the sticky Coca-Cola and glass splinters we'd left all over the floor of the pub cellar.

We closed the trapdoors, then the lorry shutters, and jumped back up into the cab without mentioning the breakages to anyone at the pub. Moments later a shattered Brendan was sitting in complete silence, staring ahead over the massive steering wheel. I didn't know what to say so I kept quiet. He looked even sicker than earlier.

'Take the wheel, son.'

For a moment, I thought I was hearing things.

'You'll be fine,' he mumbled.

And with that he jumped out of the cab and walked round the front of the Bedford towards the passenger door. I took one of my customary deep breaths and climbed over the huge gearbox cover between the two seats as he clambered in next to me. Luckily the lorry was facing southwards, down towards our next drop-off at a bar the other end of Earls Court Road.

'Let's get going, then,' said Brendan.

I checked the side mirrors and then pressed the start button and the diesel engine roared into life. We were in one of the busiest roads in London. I was fourteen years old and in charge of a seven-ton truck filled to the brim with Coca-Cola. I flicked the indicator down, shoved the stick into first gear, checked the side mirror and waited for a gap in the traffic, revving up the engine every few moments to remind myself of what I was about to do.

Just then across the road I spotted our elderly tenant Miss Hogg, the one who'd fed me so many times when my parents weren't around. She was coming out of a grocer's shop next to Earls Court Police Station, of all places. I watched her for a few moments. Then she looked up from across the street and stared right at me. I don't know why, but I waved back at her, and she smiled as if it was perfectly normal for me to be sitting in the driver's seat of a huge lorry.

Then I checked my side mirror again, noticed a gap in the traffic and let my foot gradually off the clutch, and the Bedford surged forward into the busy two-way street. I looked across at Miss Hogg one last time as I drove past her, and she was watching me, still with that slight smile on her face. She still didn't look surprised, and she never mentioned seeing me driving that lorry when I next saw her.

Suddenly I noticed a mother and baby in a pushchair crossing the zebra crossing right in front of me. I reacted swiftly and coolly and braked gently but firmly to allow them to cross. I turned and looked across at Brendan. He was slumped against the window, obviously in another world. I liked that because it meant he wasn't concerned about my driving. Basically, he was saying, 'Get on with it, son.'

Over the next two or three hundred yards I passed my mother's favourite garden centre, followed by our GP's surgery and the church hall where I was enrolled as a Boy Scout (I lasted all of fifteen minutes). I was right slap-bang in the middle of my 'home territory' and I didn't give a damn. I actually rather hoped someone would spot me.

I eased the Bedford to a halt at the traffic lights on the busy intersection with Cromwell Road, the main route west out of London. I was completely into my stride by this time. I felt confident and relaxed in control of this seven-ton truck. I kept the engines revved up at the lights because I liked the noise and the way it shook right through the cab every time I pressed on the accelerator.

CAR TROUBLE

Finally we took off from the lights and I found myself alongside a virtually identical Schweppes Bedford delivery lorry while crossing the busy intersection where Earls Court Road then became one-way. The driver and mate from the other lorry smiled across at us, and even Brendan managed to open his eyes and wave back. I felt on top of the world, eyes snapping sharply in all directions. I made sure I was aware of all other vehicles and watched my speed carefully, although I was determined to get from third to fourth gear before we reached the next Coca-Cola drop-off. I wanted to see what it was like.

I eventually got into fourth, but a few seconds later had to slow down for our next drop-off, on the corner of Earls Court Road and Old Brompton Road. I indicated and then expertly drove the Bedford up onto the kerb on the corner of the street, so we were parked as near as possible to the pub's cellar trapdoors.

Brendan seemed a little brighter now and went down to the cellar, but I could see he was still far from well. He took over the wheel again for the drive back to the depot that night, and just before I jumped out of the cab to go home, he congratulated me on my driving.

I was well chuffed by what he'd said, but my elation didn't last long. As we walked into the main depot office to submit our time sheets, the manager ordered us into his side office.

'What the fuckin' hell are you playin' at?' he yelled at Brendan. 'Apparently you let this kid drive your lorry.'

Brendan shrugged his shoulders because he was in no mood for a row. How on earth could the manager know what had happened?

'I've got you two bang to rights,' added the manager, a balding, fat-faced man with no neck who prided himself on the shine of the chrome on his company Ford Cortina.

I said nothing, but glanced across at Brendan.

'What you talkin' about?' he asked the manager.

'You were spotted, mate.'

'Bollocks,' said Brendan.

'You look like shit, Brendan. You been on the piss?'

I still didn't know what to say, but I felt the need to defend my friend and colleague.

'That's not true,' I said. At least I was trying.

'Shut yer mouth, son,' said the manager.

'Leave 'im out of it,' said Brendan.

Brendan was already on a hair trigger and this was the last straw. I felt responsible for what had happened.

'I've had enough. Fuck off.'

And with that, Brendan chucked the truck keys on the desk and stormed out.

It turned out I'd been spotted driving the lorry by a Coca-Cola 'spy' who'd been watching us to see if we were doing a fiddle with the empties. That was the end of my 'career' working for Coca-Cola. But just getting a taste of driving a truck was almost worth it.

PASSING THE CHEQUERED FLAG

THE ONLY GOOD THING ABOUT BEING FIRED FROM COCA-COLA WAS that they agreed to pay me up for the rest of the month and that gave me enough cash to go out and do what I'd been meaning to do for a long time – buy myself a car I could actually handle.

I only had about fifty quid, but in those days there were plenty of old bangers around for less than that. I picked up an *Evening Standard* and started scanning the classified section for something suitable. It had to be local because I'd have to take public transport to view it.

There was no way I was going to make the same mistake I'd made earlier when I'd bought that massive Rover Coupe. This time I'd buy a car I could afford to run and that was discreet enough not to alert anyone else to the age of the driver. That was the mistake with the Rover. There was no way a kid would drive one of them around.

Then I spotted an advert in the *Evening Standard* for a Riley 1.5, the same model as that Matchbox toy car I'd dropped in the Thames when I was three years old. It looked like a bargain at 40 quid. Nothing else in the classifieds caught my attention so I called up the owner, who was only up the road in Fulham, and I took a bus out there and offered 30 quid cash.

CAR TROUBLE

Bingo.

I now had my first proper car, and this time I wouldn't be panic-selling it back 24 hours later at a 50 per cent loss, either. I was delighted with the Riley, not least because it reminded me so much of that first childhood memory. But I did hate the beige bodywork so I bought a can of black spray paint to cover it. The Riley came with grey-leather seats, wood trim and even a rev counter, virtually unheard of in such small models when it was built in the year of my birth, 1956. But the body was more Morris Minor than Aston Martin, and its ugly backside meant I'd always reverse it out of my mates' driveways to avoid humiliation. The engine sounded as muffled as Marc Bolan eating a packet of Smith's crisps, but it was my car and that was all that mattered.

I was free at last to hit the road and do as I pleased. I'd survived, even thrived in many ways, and now I wanted to get on with my life in the real world. My trouble with cars would soon hit a new, much more dangerous phase, but now I knew what I was doing and nothing could stop me.

CAR TROUBLE

THE PROBLEM WITH HAVING MY OWN CAR AT SUCH A YOUNG AGE
was that all my mates expected me to drive them around the whole
time. I used to cart them from party to party, and on one occasion
my beer was spiked with acid in a pub and I ended up driving four
rowdy friends twenty miles to a party while so off my head that I
imagined the trees were snakes and the moon was talking to me. God
knows how I managed to avoid hitting other vehicles.

The Riley 1.5 only lasted a few months before the gearbox fell
apart, and I dumped it in a field near Weybridge, in Surrey. My next
car was an MG 1100, which cost 65 quid and served me well until
I went into the back of a lorry outside Madame Tussauds. Luckily I
managed to convince the lorry driver that it was all his fault, so we
didn't bother swapping details or calling the police.

I then bought myself a Ford Anglia, which had been 'pimped' with
a repulsive purple paint job, wide wheels and matching arches, as well
as being fitted with a Ford Corsair V4 engine. I booked a driving test
for immediately after my 17th birthday on the basis that I might as
well go legit as quickly as I could. The Anglia went like a rocket and
sounded like a racing car, but unfortunately it did not have a front
passenger seat so I took my test in a driving-school car just five days
after my 17th birthday. I sailed through the test with flying colours,

much to the irritation of the examiner, who couldn't understand how I'd learned how to drive in just five days. But I felt strangely empty when I drove home that afternoon as a legal driver for the first time in my long motoring 'career'.

No more looking nervously at police cars alongside me at traffic lights. No more late-night joyrides with cars that belonged to my friends' parents. No more sneaking round the corner to where I kept my car hidden from the adults. It was all a bit of an anticlimax now to be driving a car, whereas before it had provided an escape from my childhood. I'd got control of my life at last. I was legally in the driving seat for the first time ever.

But it's nothing short of a miracle that I even survived to tell this tale.

MY TOP TEN CHILDHOOD DRIVES

1. Jaguar 3.4 Mark II
2. Wolseley 6/110 Mark II
3. Mini Cooper
4. Triumph 2000 Mark II
5. Jaguar XJ6 2.8
6. Riley 1.5
7. Hillman Minx
8. Bedford TK lorry
9. Triumph Vitesse
10. Zodiac Mark II

A FEW FINAL WORDS

SO THERE YOU HAVE IT: A CHILDHOOD ON FOUR WHEELS. I TRIED
to go inside my head when I was growing up in order to bring you
the full flavour of my story, and it wasn't such a painful journey after
all. I'd been so concerned that the chaos that ruled my life when I
was a child might be interpreted as some kind of misery memoir that
would send readers running for the hills in search of something more
uplifting. But now I've finished writing this book, I feel as if I was
fortunate, in many ways, to have a childhood that might just provide
a bit of light entertainment for others.

The problem seems to be that when it comes to people's childhoods,
one's heart often overrules the head and so we frequently demand
more be done to make children safe, to the detriment of their
sense of adventure. We seem to want children to understand and
acknowledge the impact of their wrongdoings. We want them so
often to demonstrate genuine contrition because we want them to be
normal. But what *is* normal?

Why should children be made to change? Is that going to make them
happier and more productive? Speaking from personal experience, I
doubt it. There is such impatience in the outside world to address
their problems, as if that will make all their unhappiness just go away.
If only it was as simple as that. There are no magic pills that can

be fed to children to turn them into 'good people' or 'safe people' or 'normal people'. The only thing we can do for those children who lack a traditional upbringing with normal values is to provide compensation in the form of an alternative structured and nurturing environment.

It is certainly true that children whose lives have been chaotic and neglected feel profoundly unsafe. I felt that to a certain degree as a child. My life was, in a sense, a mask for my own vulnerability. In other words, I often believed that if I got in first then I wouldn't get so badly hurt. I probably needed to be made to feel much safer than I was, and I've certainly tried to do that with my own four children. I also could have done with a teacher who actually liked me and showed an interest in me. If that had happened, maybe I wouldn't have veered head-on into cars and the illegal activities that came with them.

Basically, I developed most of my own social and life skills so that I could engage with certain people in order to survive. Looking back on it, I know there were certain moments when I didn't really understand what I had done wrong or how I had broken 'the rules', whatever they might have been. I am not saying all this to get any sympathy. Far from it. I just want to explain some of the reasons why a lot of the stuff you have just read about happened.

Writing this book has forced me to focus on my childhood and the impact it has had on me in later life. It certainly helped me develop an awareness of how I felt about myself so that I could move on and deal with how those around me might feel. I was damaged to a certain degree, and I was certainly vulnerable, but I had this built-in radar that kept me safe, because I didn't trust anyone else.

I have tried to show where I 'was' during my childhood. I have reflected on what my childhood was all about and what my needs were back then, and found that, to a certain degree, my needs are similar now. Yet throughout all that I knew what I wanted out of life. As a child, I developed a common point of focus from which I knew certain elements would fall into place in order to give me a happy life. Now, child experts would say I needed to build my trust in other people and engage with them, but it was hard to do that when you looked after yourself from an early age.

Obviously, I didn't have the traditional boundaries, and I didn't really expect others to treat me with any respect or listen to what I had to say. But it's important to say here and now that I was not traumatised by my childhood. Of course, I was sometimes hostile and withdrawn because I had been living with inappropriate rules, parenting my parents and dealing with issues that should not have involved children. But luckily I never got anywhere near to the state that so many children brought up with real poverty, degradation and abuse all around them suffer. I didn't have it hard in the traditional sense, so it would sound pretty rich if I tried to compare myself to the 'real' childhood victims of neglect and abuse.

To many of those kids, words become virtually meaningless. They live their lives being ignored and left to their own devices only to find themselves plucked out of their homes by well-meaning social workers or whoever. Suddenly everyone is asking them questions, questions, questions. It must be so confusing.

Kids like me were loners and we survived for that very reason. I learned from an early age to deconstruct why certain situations, or other people, were not good for me. I analysed and worked things out for myself, rather than telling other people what I thought. I knew precisely what was going on around me from an early age, as well. Of course, I was quite manipulative, but that was part of my survival instinct.

I learned to interpret facial expressions in other people, although there were definitely moments when I over-interpreted hostility in others. It was easy to see anger in a neutral face sometimes. Knowing the difference between fear and sadness is not always easy when you have had few guidelines in life. In some ways I also lacked empathy as a child. I didn't really understand what it meant. Psychologists theorise that the ability to recognise fear in others comes from a childhood development stage that is critical for learning that other people are sentient, feeling organisms. They claim that such children have not developed this 'theory of mind'. Some experts who have studied this aspect of childhood development claim to have discovered that most problem children experience highly emotional states. Certainly I suffered anxiety a lot of the time, and I tended to be either completely overreactive or underreactive to things that upset me. Sometimes that meant reacting aggressively to frustrating situations. I was a child who rarely showed his emotions, except when alone, and I didn't really care about the approval of others, which is why anyone who tried to discipline me came away very frustrated. It's hardly rocket science to conclude that the more detached a child is, the less likely he is to respond to punishments for misbehaviour.

Basically I felt as if I didn't owe the world anything and I didn't like backing down from confrontations. I felt it was okay to feel angry, and my lack of an upbringing left me with the distinct impression that it was hard to get ahead without breaking the law now and again. I learned through my contact with adults how to give people the answers they might be looking for, but that was hardly surprising.

Today's trend for the pathologising of misery began with adults. Fears have become phobias and risk assessment has become paranoia. Moods have been reworded into syndromes and broken hearts have been elevated to clinical depression, leaving stoicism to trip over its own stiff upper lip in the race to oblivion. Back when I was a kid, the drug companies started tripping over themselves to provide GPs with mountains of happy pills that could be doled out to keep the blues at bay and stop annoying, neurotic patients from flooding the local surgeries. It was almost as if 'mad beat bad' every time, and people like my mother, and tens of millions of others who'd suffered a genuine personal disaster, were pushed into a convenient corner with a bottle of pills to keep them quiet. These days that's turned into a sea of self-indulgence in which everyone seems to be seeing a therapist and/or knocking back some brand or other of tranquilliser.

Today, children's unhappiness is 'diagnosed' as a 'sickness', with its attendant labels: ADHD or dysmorphia or that great old misused standby, 'depression', and of course its 'cure'. Apparently children's prescriptions for Ritalin are running at 500,000 a year and rising, while it is said that children as young as eight are being prescribed Prozac. Obviously some kids need this medication. But how on earth can the rest of these children be helped to cope with their oncoming adult life? I am glad I wasn't hauled in front of one of today's specialists because no doubt I would have been put on every type of prescription drug. As a result of witnessing my mother's vast intake of pills, I have always shied away from prescription drugs because the thought of taking anything every day repulses me. It's as if the drugs have hooked you in and there is no escape.

This might sound twisted, but my strange early years of life have convinced me that unhappiness has a rightful place in every child's life. It's part of our character development, surely? If society is obsessed with erasing it all, then when something bad does happen, how are we going to cope as adults? How can we cope with life's disappointments if we never experience unhappiness as children?

Don't get me wrong here. I know that if unhappiness rules one's life for longer than a few days, it must be dealt with, but there are experiences that children can only handle if they've been through them in some form or other.

It's important to point out that the salient details of my childhood obsession with cars may not always be 100 per cent accurate. Childhood memories can be clouded by time and emotions, so it's possible that occasionally I have veered into territory that might not completely tally with the facts. The usual point of reference is to go back to one's family to seek confirmation and accuracy, but in my case all those people are no longer alive. I openly concede that some of my strongest memories might be tainted by the way I have thought about them down the years, but the essence of my story is completely and utterly accurate: I was a child whose life revolved around cars, not people. They became my salvation, in a sense, but it has taken me all the rest of my life to fully appreciate it.

Wensley Clarkson was born in London in 1956. He left school at the age of 14 and the only exam he ever passed was his driving test, just a few days after his 17th birthday. Since 1976 he has written for a living as a journalist, author and screenwriter. He has also made several highly acclaimed TV documentaries. He lives in London and Granada, Spain, and is not related to Jeremy Clarkson.